Working

with

Computer

Type

3

The author and publisher dedicate this book to their very good friend and mentor, Jean Koefoed, without whom this series would not have been created. The recent loss of such a fine publisher and professional in the Graphic Arts field will surely be felt throughout our industry. We mourn him but rejoice in the privilege of having known and worked with him.

RC/BM 9 Oct 96

A RotoVision Book
Published and Distributed by RotoVision SA
7 rue du Bugnon
1299 Crans
Switzerland

RotoVision SA Sales Office
Sheridan House
112/116A Western Road
Hove, West Sussex BN3 1DD
England
Tel   44 1273 72 72 68
Fax   44 1273 72 72 69

Distributed to the trade in the United States by

Watson Guptill Publications
1515 Broadway
New York, New York 10036

© 1997 RotoVision SA

ISBN 2-88046-278-9

Book design by Rob Carter

Production and separations in Singapore by

ProVision Pte. Ltd.
Tel   65 334 7720
Fax   65 334 7721

Working with Computer Type

3

Rob Carter

OTOVISION

color&type

Contents

Introduction

Working with color and type poses numerous challenges. Paying attention to all of the minute but critical details in type such as typeface selection and spacing requires sensitivity, patience, and practice. When color and type join forces, the challenges are significantly magnified. Color should not only be chosen to create a desired effect or mood; it should also be chosen with typographic legibility in mind. We are accustomed to seeing black type on white paper, and traditionally this combination is most readable. From the moment color is added to either type or its background, legibility is compromised. As a result, the designer's task is to juggle the properties of both color and type, thus optimizing their communicative potential. Arm in arm, color and type are capable of breathing life into otherwise dull communication.

Prior to the onslaught of desktop computers, designers selected color from swatch-books and color charts that offered a relatively limited palette of colors. Now the designer is able to select millions of colors from electronic palettes that can be accessed instantaneously. The sheer number of color choices is overwhelming. With innumerable fonts and a tremendous number of colors available on the desktop, how does one begin the complicated process of meaningfully combining type

and color on the desktop? What factors specific to combining type and color should you consider, and how do you know when the type and color combinations you have chosen are the right ones? *Working with Computer Type: Type and Color* tackles these questions and others, offering a practical guide for art directors, graphic designers, and desktop publishers at all levels.

The book is a guide for working with color and type, as well as a practical tool for selecting color combinations for type. A panorama of type and color specimens based on basic color schemes derived from the color wheel provides an invaluable guide for selecting your own type and color combinations. 30 case studies reveal how some of the world's leading graphic designers integrate type and color, use color as a communicative element, and create color schemes for expressive and communicative purposes. While the book focuses on printed communication, the timeless concepts presented apply also to electronic and interactive applications.

Some things never change, and in the typographic realm, principles upon which sound practice relies have remained essentially the same for centuries.

me things never change, and in the typographic realm,
inciples upon which sound practice relies have remained
sentially the same for centuries. These principles have
er time developed in response to the way in which we
ad – the way in which we visually perceive the letters and
ords on a page. Working effectively with computer type
r working with type using any tool, for that matter)
quires a solid knowledge of these typographic funda-
entals. The following pages provide the reader with the
sic vocabulary needed for informed practice, and a
ller understanding and appreciation of the case studies
esented within this book.

Labels in fig. 1: arm, capline, stem, meanline, x-height, shoulder, stroke, bracket, ascender, apex, crossbar, diagonal stroke, counter, serif, baseline, descender, bowl, ear, link, loop

1

The anatomy of type

The colorful terms used to describe type are not unlike the terms used to describe the parts of our own bodies. Letters have arms, legs, eyes, spines, and a few other parts, such as tails and stems, that we fortunately do not possess. These are the parts that have historically been used to construct letterforms. Learning this vocabulary can help the designer gain appreciation for the complexity of our alphabet, which at first glance appears very simple (fig. **1**). The structure of letters within the alphabet remains constant regardless of typeface. An upper-case *B*, for example, consists of one vertical and two curved strokes. These parts, however, may be expressed very differently from typeface to typeface (fig. **2**).

BB B B B B B

eye

2

Type classification

An inexhaustible variety of type styles is available for use today, and many attempts to classify these into logical groupings have fallen short due to the overlapping visual traits of typefaces. A flawless classification system does not exist; however, a general system based on the historical development of typefaces is used widely. This delineation breaks down typefaces into the following groups: Old Style, Transitional, Modern, Slab Serif (also called Egyptian), Sans Serif, and Display (fig. **3**).

Old Style characteristics:
Medium stroke contrast
Slanted stress
Oblique, bracketed serifs
Medium overall weight

Transitional characteristics:
Medium to high stroke contrast
Nearly vertical stress
Sharp, bracketed serifs
Slightly slanted serifs

Modern characteristics:
High stroke contrast
Vertical stress
Thin serifs
Serifs sometimes unbracketed

Egyptian characteristics:
Little stroke contrast
Little or no stress
Thick, square serifs
Large x-height

Sans serif characteristics:
Some stroke contrast
Nearly vertical stress
Squarish, curved strokes
Lower-case *g* has open tail

Display typefaces do not possess a fixed number of characteristics.

Old Style

Transitional

Modern

Slab serif

Sans serif

Display

leg
foot
tail

3

The typographic font

In desktop publishing, the terms typeface and font are often used synonymously; however, a typeface is the design of characters unified by consistent visual properties, while a font is the complete set of characters in any one design, size, or style of type. These characters include but are not limited to upper- and lower-case

spine

...ters, numerals, small capitals, fractions, liga-
...es (two or more characters linked together
...o a single unit), punctuation, mathematical
...ns, accents, monetary symbols, and miscel-
...eous dingbats (assorted ornaments or
...urons designed for use in a font). Supple-
...enting some desktop fonts are expert sets,
...ich include characters such as small caps, a
...od selection of ligatures, fractions, and
...naligning figures. Minion Regular provides
...excellent example of a font and its attendant
...pert set (fig. **4**).

...e type family

...type family is a group of typefaces bound
...gether by similar visual characteristics.
...embers of a family (typefaces) resemble one
...other, but also have their own unique visual
...aits. Typefaces within families consist of
...fferent weights and widths. Some type fami-
...s consist of many members; others are
...mposed of just a few. Extended families such
...Stone include both serif and sans serif
...riations (fig. **5**).

...ypographic measurement

...e two primary units of measure in typog-
...phy are the pica and the point. There are
...pproximately six picas or 72 points to an inch;
...ere are twelve points to a pica (fig. **6**). Points
...e used to specify the size of type, which
...cludes the cap height of letters, plus a small
...terval of space above and below the letters.
...ypefaces of the same size may in fact appear
...fferent in size, depending on the size of the
...height. At the same size, letters with large
...-heights appear larger than letters with smaller
...-heights. Points are also used to measure the
...stance between lines; picas are used to
...easure the lengths of lines. The unit, a relative
...easure determined by dividing the em (which
...the square of the type size), is used to reduce
...r increase the amount of space between

---

abcdefghijklmnopqrstuvwxyz
ABCDEFGHIJKLMNOPQRSTUVWXYZ&
ABCDEFGHIJKLMNOPQRSTUVWXYZ&
(.,;:,!?""''~''~~\\//..^^~ ~''' «»‹›- – —)
1234567890 1234567890 ($^{1234567890}/_{1234567890}$)
¼⅓½⅔¾⅝⅞%‰ [+√π=≠±≤≥÷∞°]
fffiflffifflŒßæœ $£§¢
ÂÅÁÇÍÎÏØÓÒÔÚ áéíóúåäëïöüàèìòùâêîû
¶‡†•*∧ ©™@

4

Stone Serif

Regular
Regular Italic
Semibold
Semibold Italic
Bold
Bold Italic

Stone Sans

Regular
Regular Italic
Semibold
Semibold Italic
Bold
Bold Italic

5

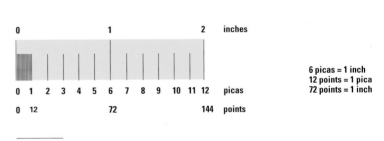

6 picas = 1 inch
12 points = 1 pica
72 points = 1 inch

6

---

letters, a process called tracking. Adjusting the
awkward space between two letters to create
consistency within words is called kerning.

The typographic grid

A typographic grid is used to aid the designer
in organizing typographic and pictorial elements on a page and establishing unity among
all of the parts of a design. Grids vary in com-

Legibility

plexity and configuration depending upon the nature of the information needing accommodation, and the physical properties of the typographic elements. Standard typographic grids possess flow lines, grid modules, text columns, column intervals, and margins (fig. **7**).

If the goal when working with type is to make it more readable, then heeding established legibility guidelines is of utmost importance. Departure from these "rules" should be attempted only after a designer is totally familiarized with them, and when content lends itself to expressive interpretation. Legibility represents those visual attributes in typography that make type readable.

Choosing typefaces

The first step in making type legible is to choose text typefaces that are open and well proportioned, typefaces that exhibit the regularity of classical serif faces, such as Baskerville, Bembo, Bodoni, Garamond; and the sans serif faces Franklin Gothic, Frutiger, and Gill Sans (fig. **8**). Typefaces with visual quirks, stylistic affectations, and irregularities among characters are less legible. Typefaces such as these may be fine, however, when used as display type.

flow line
grid modules
text columns
column intervals
margins

7

Serif	Sans serif
Bembo	Franklin Gothic
Baskerville	Frutiger
Bodoni	Futura
Century Expanded	Gill Sans
Garamond	Helvetica

8

Type size, line length, and line spacing

Text that flows naturally when read is achieved when a harmonious relationship exists between type size, line length, and the spaces between lines of type (line spacing or leading). Even well-designed typefaces suffer from legibility impairment when just one of these aspects is out of balance. An adjustment to one of these factors usually requires an adjustment to one or more of the others.

ntinuous text type that is too large or too

all easily tires the reader. Optimum sizes for

t type are between 8 and 11 points. Also,

efaces with a relatively large x-height

prove readability.

erly long or short lines of type also tire the

der and destroy a pleasant reading rhythm.

ng lines are burdensome and tedious,

ereas short lines cause choppy eye move-

ents. Paying attention to the number of

aracters per line is a key in determining

propriate line lengths. It is generally agreed

at lines of type consisting of a maximum of

ty or seventy characters promote readability

. **9**).

e spacing ensures that the reader is not

tracted by lines of type that visually run

ether. Without adequate space between

es, the eye struggles to distinguish one line

m the next. Where lines are too widely

aced, the reader has trouble locating the next

e. For optimum sizes of text type (8-11

ints), one to four points of line spacing can

lp the reader easily discern each line, thus

proving readability (fig. **10**).

8/9

Line spacing ensures that the reader is not distracted by lines of type that visually run together. With inadequate space between lines, the eye struggles to distinguish one line from the next. Where lines are too widely spaced, the reader has trouble locating the next line. For optimum sizes of text type (8-11 points), one to four points of line

8/11

Line spacing ensures that the reader is not distracted by lines of type that visually run together. With inadequate space between lines, the eye struggles to distinguish one line from the next. Where lines are too widely spaced, the reader has trouble locating the next line. For

---

8/10

Line spacing ensures that the reader is not distracted by lines of type that visually run together. With inadequate space between lines, the eye struggles to distinguish one line from the next. Where lines are too widely spaced, the reader has trouble locating the next line. For optimum sizes of text type (8-11

8/12

Line spacing ensures that the reader is not distracted by lines of type that visually run together. With inadequate space between lines, the eye struggles to distinguish one line from the next. Where lines are too widely spaced, the reader has trouble locating the next line. For

---

10

Overly long or short lines of type also tire the reader and destroy a pleasant reading rhythm. Long lines are burdensome and tedious, whereas short lines cause choppy eye movements. Paying attention to the number of characters per line is a key in determining appropriate line lengths. It is generally agreed that lines of type consisting of a maximum of sixty or seventy characters promote readability.

Overly long or short lines of type also tire the reader and destroy a pleasant reading rhythm. Long lines are burdensome and tedious, whereas short lines cause choppy eye movements. Paying attention to the number of characters per line is a key in determining appropriate line lengths. It is

Letter spacing

A number of factors determines correct letter spacing, including the typeface used, and the size and weight of the type. Consistent letter spacing provides an even typographic "color," a term referring to the texture and overall lightness or darkness of text. Consistent and even color is an attribute that enhances readability. Tighter letter spacing darkens the text, as in this sentence. L o o s e r l e t t e r s p a c i n g l i g h t e n s t h e t e x t. Pushed to either extreme, text becomes less readable. The chosen effect can enliven a page and enhance communication.

Word spacing

Word spacing should be proportionally adjusted to letter spacing so that letters flow gracefully and rhythmically into words, and words into lines. Too much word spacing destroys the even texture desired in text and causes words to become disjointed, as in this sentence. Too little word spacing causes words to bump into one another. Either condition is hard on the reader.

Weight

The overall heaviness or lightness of the strokes composing type can affect readability. For typefaces that are too heavy, counters fill in and disappear. Typefaces that are too light are not easily distinguished from their background. Typefaces of contrasting weight are effectively used to create emphasis within text.

Width

Narrow typefaces are effectively used where there is an abundance of text, and space must be preserved. But readability is diminished when letters are too narrow (condensed) or too wide (expanded). Condensed letters fit nicely into narrow columns.

Italics

Italic and oblique type should be used with prudence, for large amounts of slanted characters set into text impede reading. Italics are best suited to create emphasis within text rather than to function as text.

Capitals versus lower case

TEXT SET IN ALL CAPITAL LETTERS NOT ONLY CONSUMES MORE SPACE THAN TEXT SET IN LOWER CASE, IT SEVERELY RETARDS THE READING PROCESS. LOWER-CASE LETTERS IMBUE TEXT WITH VISUAL CUES CREATED BY AN ABUNDANCE OF LETTER SHAPES, ASCENDERS, DESCENDERS, AND IRREGULAR WORD SHAPES. TEXT SET IN ALL CAPITALS IS VOID OF THESE CUES, FOR IT LACKS THIS VISUAL VARIETY.

serif versus sans serif

Because of the horizontal flow created by serifs, it was thought at one time that serif typefaces were more readable than sans serif typefaces. Legibility research, however, reveals little difference between them. Sensitive letter spacing is a more important consideration.

justified versus unjustified

Text can be aligned in five different ways: flush left, ragged right; flush right, ragged left; justified; centered; asymmetrically.

Flush left, ragged right text produces very even letter and word spacing, and because lines of type terminate at different points, the reader is able to easily locate each new line. This is perhaps the most legible means of aligning text.

Flush right, ragged left alignments work against the reader by making it difficult to find each new line. This method is suitable for small amounts of text, but is not recommended for large amounts.

Justified text (text aligned both left and right) can be very readable if the designer ensures that the spacing between letters and words is consistent, and that awkward gaps called "rivers" do not interrupt the flow of the text. Desktop publishing software enables the designer to fine tune the spacing.

Centered alignments give the text a very formal appearance and are fine when used minimally. But setting large amounts of text in this way should be avoided.

Asymmetrical alignments
are used when the designer
wishes to

break
the text down into logical   "thought units,"

or to give the page
a more expressive appearance.
Obviously,
setting large amounts of text
in this manner

will tire the reader.

Color is visual magic, a language of illusion. Color is also reflected light, and as lighting conditions change, so does color. This explains why as night falls colors fade, and why the colors of a landscape vary significantly when viewed at different times of the day.

or is visual magic, a language of illusion. Color is also
ected light, and as lighting conditions change, so does
or. This explains why as night falls colors fade, and why
colors of a landscape vary significantly when viewed at
erent times of the day. When we see a color, what we
ually see is an object that absorbs certain wavelengths of
t and reflects others back to our eyes. For example, a red
ect absorbs all of the light rays except the red rays which
filtered back to the eyes. Black objects absorb all of the
t rays, reflecting none back to our eyes; white objects
sorb no rays, reflecting all of them back to our eyes. This
enomenon was first revealed in 1666 by Isaac Newton
o found that by passing a beam of white light through a
sm, he could break it up into the familiar spectrum of
nbow colors: violet, indigo, blue, green, yellow, orange,
d red. We are most familiar with this spectrum, and the
man eye easily perceives it. In reality, the spectral colors
sist of a vast array of hues, each corresponding to a
cific wavelength of light.

s chapter reviews basic color theory, and defines impor-
t color terms. For the beginner, it lays a solid foundation
building a deeper knowledge of color. For the profes-
nal designer and desktop publisher, it provides a wel-
me review. Learning to see color and obtaining an
derstanding of its inherent properties are the first steps to
rking effectively with color and type.

The color wheel

The color wheel is a helpful tool that shows the basic organization and interrelationships of colors. It is also used as a tool for color selection. This color wheel provides basic color terminology that anyone working with type and color should be completely familiar with. Many color wheel models exist, and some are quite complex. This wheel consists of 12 basic colors (fig. 1). It is conceivable for a wheel to consist of an infinite number of variations, too subtle for the human eye to discern. Contained within the circle of color is a square of black, which is obtained by mixing together all of the surrounding colors. Though this color wheel consists of only 12 colors, it is the root of all other colors, a pure statement of chromatic harmony, and a fountain of imagination and emotion.

1

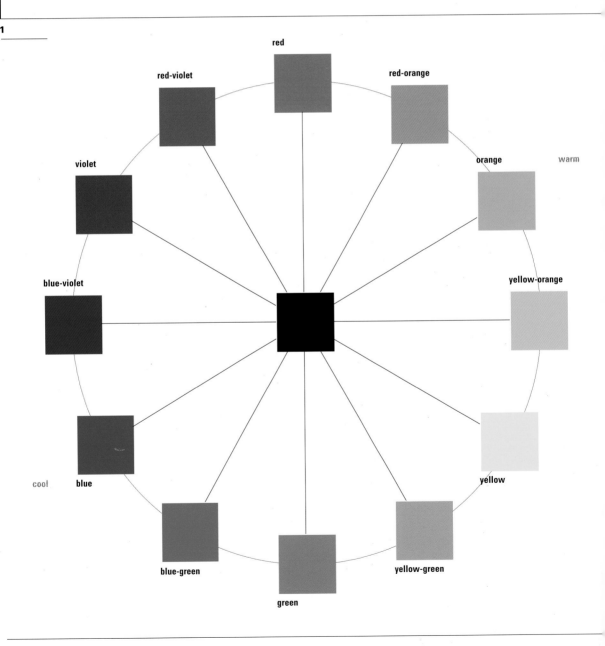

hue

hue

hue

Three different sets of primary hues are accepted for use in different disciplines. The first set consists of red, yellow and blue and is used by artists and designers. Pigments of these colors can be mixed to obtain all other colors (top). The second set of primaries are red, green and blue. Called the additive primaries, these are the primaries of light and are used in science. These are also the colors found on the computer screen. When these colors are added together in different amounts they form all other colors; when added together equally they produce white light (middle). The third set consists of magenta, yellow, and cyan. These are the subtractive primaries and are used by printers. In printing, color separations are made by using filters to subtract light from the additive primaries, resulting in the subtractive process printing colors (bottom).

3

is simply another name for color. The pure
s are identified by familiar names such as
violet, green, purple, yellow. In the world of
mercial products and pigments, hues have
n given thousands of names. Desert Rose,
ter, Woodland Green, Apache Red, and
can Violet may evoke romantic and exotic
ughts, but these names, aside from their
keting value, have little to do with the
position of the colors they represent. In
ity, few legitimate names exist for hues. The
ic twelve-color wheel pictured on the
osite page features the primary hues red,
ow, and blue; the secondary hues orange,
en, and violet; and the six tertiary hues red-
nge, orange-yellow, yellow-green, blue-

green, blue-violet, and red-violet (fig. **2**). The
secondary hues are obtained by mixing equal
amounts of two primaries; the tertiary hues are
acquired by mixing equal amounts of a primary
and an adjacent secondary hue. Complementary colors are opposite hues on the color
wheel, such as red and green, violet and yellow.
Due to the vast range of reds, yellows, and
blues, not all color wheels introduce the same
primary hues (fig. **3**). Primaries are considered
absolute colors and cannot be created by
mixing other colors together. However, mixing
the primaries into various combinations creates
an infinite number of colors.

ary hues

Secondary hues

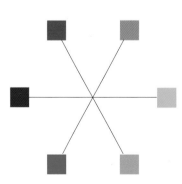

Tertiary hues

Value

Value refers to the lightness or darkness of a color. It is a variable that can substantially alter a color's appearance, and as we will see in the next chapter, it is also an important factor in achieving legibility with type and color. A hue changes in value when either white or black are added to it. A color with added white is called a tint (fig. **4**); a color with added black is called a shade (fig. **5**). Generally speaking, pure hues that are normally light in value (yellow, orange, green) make the best tints, while pure hues that are normally dark in value (red, blue, violet) make the most desirable shades. The palette of colors below shows a spectrum of tints and shades based on the hues from the color wheel (fig. **6**). Looking at these colors clearly shows that changes in value greatly expand color possibilities. The bottom row (fig. **7**), consisting of the achromatic colors white, black, and gray, is presented in increments of 10%.

1 2 3 4 5 6 7 8 9 10 11 12

Twelve basic hues

6

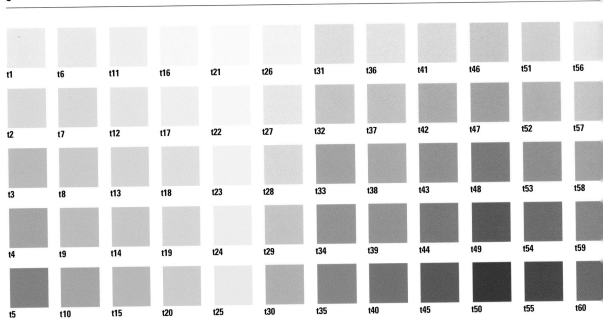

t1 t6 t11 t16 t21 t26 t31 t36 t41 t46 t51 t56
t2 t7 t12 t17 t22 t27 t32 t37 t42 t47 t52 t57
t3 t8 t13 t18 t23 t28 t33 t38 t43 t48 t53 t58
t4 t9 t14 t19 t24 t29 t34 t39 t44 t49 t54 t59
t5 t10 t15 t20 t25 t30 t35 t40 t45 t50 t55 t60

Tints

4

ote about the color used in this book.
process colors below include five tints of
h pure hue on the color wheel, five shades,
d the achromatic hues for a total of 143
ors. The colors are numbered for reference
the type and color combinations in chapter 4,
d the case studies in chapter 5. This color
lette could be expanded to include the most
otle variations, but quantity of colors is not
most important consideration. While in fact

this palette offers hundreds of color possibilities, it is far more critical to learn to control
color as it is used for typographic applications,
and to develop a sensitive eye. When it comes
to working with color and type, less is more. A
CMYK conversion chart for the colors is located
on page 154.

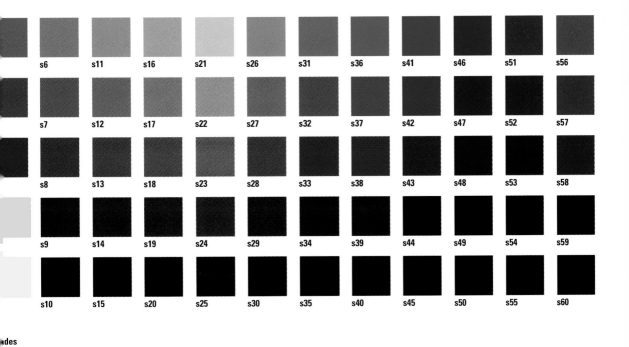

s6 s11 s16 s21 s26 s31 s36 s41 s46 s51 s56

s7 s12 s17 s22 s27 s32 s37 s42 s47 s52 s57

s8 s13 s18 s23 s28 s33 s38 s43 s48 s53 s58

s9 s14 s19 s24 s29 s34 s39 s44 s49 s54 s59

s10 s15 s20 s25 s30 s35 s40 s45 s50 s55 s60

des

k1 k2 k3 k4 k5 k6 k7 k8 k9 k10

hromatic colors

Saturation

Also called chroma or intensity, saturation refers to the brightness of a hue. The highest saturation occurs in colors that are pure and unmixed. Any color mixture will diminish intensity. However, adding white, gray, black, or a complementary color most radically compromises intensity (fig. **8**). Variations of a single hue dulled in intensity by different amounts of an added complement are often referred to as tones. When complementary colors are placed in close proximity, the intensity of each is increased. This vibrant condition is referred to as simultaneous contrast (fig. **9**).

Color temperature

The terms "warm" and "cool" are used to express those hues that connote these respective qualities. In general, reds, oranges, and yellows "feel" warm, while blues, greens, and purples "feel" cool. Distinctions between warm and cool colors can be very subtle. For example, white paper can appear either warmer or cooler depending upon the slight influence of red or blue. The same applies to gray and black (fig. **10**).

a a a a a

These five letters demonstrate the principle of color saturation. The first letter is fully saturated and is the brightest. The second letter has added black and is darker; the third letter has white added to it and is lighter; the fourth contains red, the complement of green, and is darker and duller; the fifth letter has added blue and appears duller than the fully saturated color.

8

Two fully saturated and complementary colors vibrate as a result of simultaneous contrast.

9

warm
warmer
hot

Red, orange, and yellow are colors that suggest warmth. Colors appear hotter as yellow decreases and as red increases.

cool
cooler
cold

Blue, turquoise, and green are cool colors; blue is very cold. Green is slightly warmer due to the addition of yellow.

warm gray
cool gray

Warm gray contains a small percentage of red while cool gray casts a slight blue.

10

eeing color

erhaps the most important concept to realize
oout color is that it is conditional. No single
olor can be judged outside of its environment.
olors physically affect one another. We owe a
ebt to Josef Albers, an influential artist,
esigner, and educator who first developed a
eory based on his observations about the
lativity of color. His writings have pivotally
fluenced artists and designers for half a
entury. In his book *Interaction of Color* he
ates, "First, it should be learned that one and
e same color evokes innumerable readings."
e demonstrates that the same color can
opear very different when placed on different
ackgrounds, and that different colors can
opear nearly the same when juxtaposed with
fferent backgrounds. In addition to changes in
ue, colors are influenced in terms of lightness
nd darkness, warmness and coolness, and
rightness and dullness, depending upon
urrounding colors. When working with color
nd type, it is important to be aware of all the
vays in which color contrasts can be accom-
lished. Albers advocated an active, experi-
ental approach to color, one of practice
efore theory. The only way to truly see and
nderstand a color is to observe it in relation-
nip to its environment. In this sense, color can
e "read" by designers and applied with
ensitivity and sound judgment. The examples
n this page reveal the interdependent nature
f color (fig. **11**).

The two letters to the left are identical in color. Placing them on two different backgrounds makes them appear different in both hue and value. The dark green background absorbs green from the left *a*, leaving it lighter and more yellow. Conversely, the bright yellow background absorbs yellow from the right *a*, leaving it darker and bluer.

Two identical warm red letters appear very different on different backgrounds. The warm background makes the left letter *a* appear cooler, while the cool background of the right letter *a* accentuates the letter's warmth.

Though these two letters are the same color, a light background makes the letter *a* on the left appear less bright than the letter *a* on the right, which has a dark background.

Color transparency

When working with color and type, it is important to establish color harmony, a condition resulting both from the choice of colors and their order in the visual field. Black, white, and gray always form a harmonious relationship because they resemble each other. Harmony is enhanced, however, when the sequence progresses naturally from black to gray to white (fig. **12**). Just as artists mix paints to create new colors, designers working with a computer can "mix" colors by selecting mixtures from available color palettes. Color mixing is simply finding relationships among colors. Mixing two colors to form a third, for example, creates a visual bridge between the first two colors. The third color is an offspring hue resembling both parents. Placing a mixed color between two parent colors is not only a harmonious ordering of the hues, it creates the surprising illusion of transparency. The original two colors appear as sheets of colored acetate that overlap and form a third color (fig. **13**). The ability to find similarities among colors is an important part of the color selection process, for it provides a way of achieving harmony and concordance among all the colors in a design.

Black to gray to white forms a natural and harmonious sequence.

12

One is able to see just a subtle hint of the red-violet as the rather opaque light yellow overlaps it.

A dark and light version of a hue combine to form a medium version of the hue.

The intense red is just transparent enough to allow the light yellow to peek through it.

The green appears to overlap and darken the blue.

13

The color triangle

The color triangle is a diagram that shows the interrelationships of hue, black, and white, and the intermediate tints, shades, and gray (fig. 14). Selecting colors along any axis of the triangle will generally result in harmonious combinations. It is important to realize that black, white, and hue are absolute, and that tints, shades, and grays possess innumerable variations. The axes shown with bold lines represent combinations that are very effective for use with type and background. Below, a few examples of the color triangle illustrate harmonious color combinations (fig. 15).

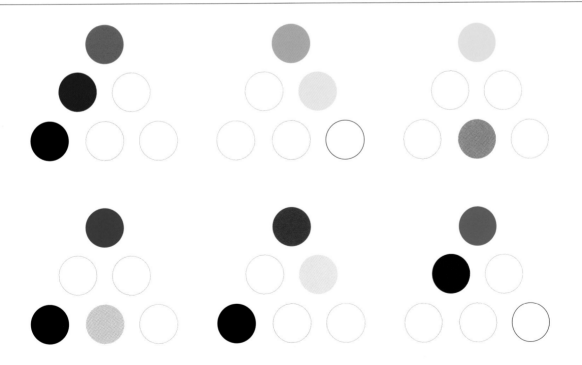

The basic color schemes

The color schemes below provide models for the exploration of harmonious, inventive, and communicative color combinations fig. **16**). All of these schemes are based upon the physical laws, relationships, and inherent structure of the color wheel. It is significant that these color formulations are at the heart of the chromatic displays found in nature: red desert sandstone glowing against a deep indigo sky; the variegated green perennial garden, accented with crimson blooms. The basic color schemes are at the root of most effective color combinations and may be used alone or combined into more elaborate combinations. An understanding of these schemes is essential when working with color and type, for they provide a departure point for further color investigation. When used

Primary
A combination of the primary hues, red, yellow, and blue, these colors are elemental and pure.

Secondary
Any combination of the secondary colors violet, orange, and green, and their tints and shades.

Tertiary
Any combination of the eight tertiary colors: red-orange, yellow-green, blue-violet, blue-green, yellow-orange, and red-violet. These hybrid colors fall between the primaries and secondaries on the color wheel.

Monochromatic
Consists of any single hue and its tints and shades

Achromatic
Combinations of black, white, and gray hues.

16

ith type, color should always be chosen for its
sual appeal as well as for its ability to com-
unicate and promote typographic legibility.
ith the aid of these basic schemes, you can
nture daringly into uncharted terrain to
eate color combinations that are both func-
onal and emotionally charged. Color is bold,
oft, energetic, somber, feminine, masculine,
endy, and traditional. A limitless

communicator, color is capable of expressing
the richness of culture, or portraying something
as exciting as a calypso dance or as musty as a
smoky restaurant. The case studies found in
chapter 5 demonstrate how the basic color
schemes can be expanded and adapted in creative typographic designs.

To provide a mental picture
of the relative locations of
colors on the color wheel,
small color wheel diagrams,
such as the one pictured
here, accompany the
schemes on this spread and
in the color combinations in
chapter 4. Compare these to
the actual color wheel on
page 18.

mplementary
scheme comprising any
o colors and their tints and
ades that are directly
posite one another on the
lor wheel.

lit complementary
juxtaposition of any hue
d the two colors located
either side of its
mplement.

alogous
nsists of a combination of
lors that are adjacent to
e another on the color
heel.

eutral
hue combined with a
rcentage of its
mplement or black.

congruous
fbeat combinations con-
sting of a hue and a color
the right or left of its
mplement.

When color and type are combined, the visual as well as the emotional attributes of type are enhanced. At the same time, changing the color of type or its back-ground can signifi-cantly affect legibility.

Color and type

When color and type are combined, the visual as well as the emotional attributes of type are enhanced. At the same time, changing the color of type or its background can significantly affect legibility. How readable you decide type should be depends upon the intent of your message. When working with color and type, remember that the following guidelines are just that . . . *guidelines* to be tested and adapted to suit the unique needs of the typographic message.

A matter of contrast

Bodoni is a refined, crisp typeface designed in the 18th century. It is at its best when presented in black on white. The extreme thick and thin relationship of its strokes are compromised when printed in any other color combination. Compare Bodoni set in three different color combinations.

Bodoni

Bodoni

Bodoni

1

Black type on a white background is easiest to read. Notice how the gray background diminishes legibility. Reversing type to appear white on black inverts the contrast relationship, making the type less legible. Although reversing type is common practice, it is not advisable to set large amounts of text in this manner.

Black type on a white background is easiest to read. Notice how as backgrounds become darker in tone, legibility diminishes.

Black type on a white background is easiest to read. Notice how as backgrounds become darker in tone, legibility diminishes.

Black type on a white background is easiest to read. Notice how as backgrounds become darker in tone, legibility diminishes.

2

The impact of hue, value, and saturation on legibility

Legible typography possesses attributes that make it readable, and if attaining typographic readability is a priority, as most often it should be, a number of important factors must be juggled. These include the choice of typeface; type size; type weight; and letter, word, and line spacing (see chapter 1). When color is applied to type, the interplay of hue, value, and saturation must be considered.

Most typefaces are designed to be read as black letters on a white ground, and they achieve optimum legibility printed in this manner (fig. **1**). There is nothing ambiguous about black and white. They are completely balanced opposites, offering exquisite contrast. When reading large amounts of type, the contrast of black on white is what readers are most accustomed to (fig. **2**).

Type presented in the highly saturated blue and orange combination is very difficult to read. Adjusting the value of either the type or the background greatly improves legibility.

Type presented in the highly saturated blue and orange combination is very difficult to read. Adjusting the value of either the type or the background greatly improves legibility. Compare the legibility of the two top and the two bottom text blocks.

Type presented in the highly saturated blue and orange combination is very difficult to read. Adjusting the value of either the type or the background greatly improves legibility.

Type presented in the highly saturated blue and orange combination is very difficult to read. Adjusting the value of either the type or the background greatly improves legibility.

Type presented in the highly saturated blue and orange combination is very difficult to read. Adjusting the value of either the type or the background greatly improves legibility.

e most important thing you can do to hieve optimum legibility when working with or and type is to carefully weigh the three or properties to establish appropriate con- st between letters and their background. All ors possess a definable hue, value, and ensity by their very nature. When combining or and type, balancing these characteristics critical.

3

us look at a couple of examples. The fully urated, complementary colors blue and nge offer plenty of hue contrast, but when lied to type and background the edges of erforms tend to vibrate, creating a turbing kinetic effect that quickly numbs the es and tires the reader. Both of these colors ssess a competing brightness, fighting for ention. If one of these hues is "softened" or ushed back" by making it lighter or darker in ue (selecting a tint or shade of the hue), the e becomes much more legible (fig. **3**). In a ferent example, two saturated, analogous ors such as blue and green provide sufficient trast without a disturbing, dizzying effect. cause the green appears both lighter and ghter than the blue, there may be no need further adjustment (fig. **4**). If analogous ors are too close to each other on the color eel and if they do not provide enough hue or ue contrast, adjustments should be made to rpen the contrast (fig. **5**).

Blue and yellow-green hues seem to work well here. Even so, if the value of the yellow-green is tweaked slightly, legibility improves.

Blue and yellow-green hues seem to work well here. Even so, if the value of the yellow-green is tweaked slightly, legibility improves.

Blue and yellow-green hues seem to work well here. Even so, if the value of the yellow-green is tweaked slightly, legibility improves.

4

Red and orange, analogous colors close to each other on the color wheel, do not provide sufficient contrast for adequate legibility. Using a tint of the orange great- ly improves the situation.

Red and orange, analogous colors close to each other on the color wheel, do not pro- vide sufficient contrast for good legibility. Using a tint of the orange greatly improves the situation.

Red and orange, analogous colors close to each other on the color wheel, do not provide sufficient contrast for adequate legibility. Using a tint of the orange great- ly improves the situation.

5

Of all the contrasts of color, value can be used to enhance legibility most significantly. Value contrasts effectively preserve the shapes and integrity of letters, making them more easily recognizable.

A good rule of thumb is to choose colors not directly across from one another, nor too close to one another on the color wheel. There will, of course, always be exceptions. Look for compatible colors but colors which also differ in value and intensity. If you must use a combination of hues that for some reason do not meet legibility standards, try improving them by turning value or intensity up or down.

Typeface and color

Every typeface possesses unique qualities that should be taken into consideration when choosing color. These qualities include proportion, weight, width, presence or absence

Some typefaces are less legible than others, even when printed in black on white and with optimum sizing and spacing. This is due to differences in design. Letters with extreme proportions (heavy, light, wide, or thin) or letters with visually challenging shapes are more difficult to read when color is added. Choose color combinations that preserve the integrity of such typefaces. Compare the problematic examples on the left with examples on the right that incorporate proper color adjustments.

Some typefaces are less legible than others, even when printed in black on white and with optimum sizing and spacing. This is due to differences in design.

Some typefaces are less legible than others, even when printed in black on white and with optimum sizing and spacing. This is due to differences in design.

Some typefaces are less legible than others, even when printed in black on white and with optimum sizing and spacing. This is due to differences in design.

Some typefaces are less legible than others, even when printed in black on white and with optimum sizing and spacing. This is due to differences in design.

Some typefaces are less legible than others, even when printed in black on white and with optimum sizing and spacing. This is due to differences in design.

Some typefaces are less legible than others, even when printed in black on white and with optimum sizing and spacing. This is due to differences in design.

Some typefaces are less legible than others, even when printed in black on white and with optimum sizing and spacing. This is due to differences in design.

Some typefaces are less legible than others, even when printed in black on white and with optimum sizing and spacing. This is due to differences in design.

6

serifs, and eccentricities in typeface design. ...very thin or narrow typeface, a peculiar or ...namental face, or a script may appear very ...ak and illegible if hues are too similar or if ...lues are too close. Enough contrast must ...ist to preserve the fidelity of the letterforms ...g. **6**).

...pographic "color"

...ack and white are neutral colors. When type ...printed in black or any other color, each

separate type design possesses a different tone (figs. **7, 8**). This effect is sometimes referred to as typographic "color." Creating different tones for different parts of a text is important, for it is in this way that hierarchical order and emphasis are achieved. This principle is demonstrated in the text that you are now reading; the main text appears lighter, and the subheads appear darker though both are printed in black.

...ice the differences in the "color" of these ... text blocks. Though only two actual colors ... used (black and red), each block of text ...pears different from every other block.

Notice the differences in the "color" of these ten text blocks. Though only two actual colors are used (black and red), each block of text appears different from every other block.

...tice the differences in the "color" of ...se ten text blocks. Though only two ...ual colors are used (black and red), ...ch block of text appears different from ...ery other block.

Notice the differences in the "color" of these ten text blocks. Though only two actual colors are used (black and red), each block of text appears different from every other block.

...tice the differences in the "color" ...these ten text blocks. Though only ...o actual colors are used (black and ...), each block of text appears ...ferent from every other block.

Notice the differences in the "color" of these ten text blocks. Though only two actual colors are used (black and red), each block of text appears different from every other block.

...e the differences in the "color" of these ten text blocks. Though only two ...colors are used (black and red), each block of text appears different from ...other block.

Notice the differences in the "color" of these ten text blocks. Though only two actual colors are used (black and red), each block of text appears different from every other block.

...TICE THE DIFFERENCES IN THE "COLOR" OF ...SE TEN TEXT BLOCKS. THOUGH ONLY TWO ...UAL COLORS ARE USED (BLACK AND RED), ...H BLOCK OF TEXT APPEARS DIFFERENT FROM ...RY OTHER BLOCK.

NOTICE THE DIFFERENCES IN THE "COLOR" OF THESE TEN TEXT BLOCKS. THOUGH ONLY TWO ACTUAL COLORS ARE USED (BLACK AND RED), EACH BLOCK OF TEXT APPEARS DIFFERENT FROM EVERY OTHER BLOCK.

Notice the differences in the "color" of these ten text blocks. Though only two actual colors are used (black and red), each block of text appears different in color from every other block. This effect is a visual illusion created by the proportions and shapes of the typeface designs.

color

color

color

The principle of typographic "color" is also true of larger display type. Though these three words are all printed in black, each possesses a different tone due to the unique characteristics of the individual typeface designs.

Type spacing and color

Letter, word, and line spacing also affect type color. Words appear lighter in tone if letters are positioned further apart (fig. **9**). Likewise, as word and line spacing increase, type appears lighter in value (fig. **10**). Paying attention to the spacing needs of type as discussed in chapter **1** can greatly improve legibility when color contrasts are marginal or when large amounts of text must be set in color (fig. **11**).

Type size and color

Small type, type that is light in weight, and delicately proportioned type with serifs suffer greatly when contrast in hue or value is insufficient (fig. **12**). As type decreases in size, color contrast must increase in strength.

As letter spacing increases, words appear lighter in tone.

color   color
color   color
color   color

9

You can achieve the illusion of darker or lighter text blocks as you decrease or increase interline spacing. Even if you are limited to the use of one color, you can create the appearance of several colors.

You can achieve the illusion of darker or lighter text blocks as you decrease or increase interline spacing. Even if limited to the use of one color, you can create the appearance of several colors.

You can achieve the illusion of darker or lighter text blocks as you decrease or increase interline spacing. Even if limited to the use of one color, you can create the appearance of several colors.

You can achieve the illusion of darker or lighter text blocks as you decrease or increase interline spacing. Even if limited to the use of one color, you can create the appearance of several colors.

10

If you find it necessary to present large amounts of text type in color, try increasing slightly the amount of space between lines. Even an additional point of space can make a significant difference, and a reader might be encouraged to continue rather than stop.

If you find it necessary to present large amounts of text type in color, try increasing slightly the amount of space between lines. Even an additional point of space can make a significant difference, and a reader might be encouraged to continue rather than stop

If you find it necessary to present large amounts of text type in an elaborate color setting, try increasing slightly the amount of space between lines. Even an additional point of space can make a significant difference, helping a reader to more easily find the next line while reading.

11

The smaller and more delicate the type, the more value and intensity contrast is needed to ensure adequate legibility.

The smaller and more delicate the type, the more value and intensity contrast is needed to ensure adequate legibility.

The smaller and more delicate the type, the more value and intensity contrast is needed to ensure adequate legibility.

The smaller and more delicate the type, the more value and intensity contrast is needed to ensure adequate legibility.

12

A background texture can interfere with the type if it is too busy, loud, and abrasive. Make a color adjustment, if necessary, to uphold the type's integrity.

A background texture can interfere with the type if it is too busy, loud, and abrasive. Make a color adjustment, if necessary, to uphold the type's integrity.

A background texture can interfere with the type if it is too busy, loud, and abrasive. Make a color adjustment, if necessary, to uphold the type's integrity.

13

...pe on busy backgrounds

...sy backgrounds or textured backgrounds
...mpete with the legibility of type. When plac-
...g type onto or reversing type from textured
...ckgrounds, make certain there is plenty of
...ntrast to maintain legibility (fig. **13**). When
...mbining type with photographs, find a quiet
...ce within the photo that will not compro-
...se the type, or insert the type within a separ-
...e overlapping background.

...reening type

...reening type is a way to expand color
...tions without actually having to pay for addi-
...nal colors. Screens are particularly effective
... one- and two-color printing jobs. Type can
... printed as a screen or reversed from a
...eened background. The percentage of the
...een affects the legibility of the type (fig. **14**).

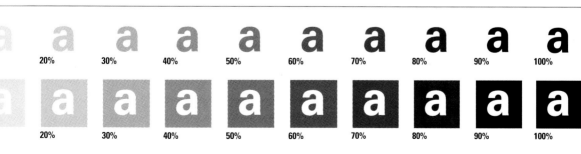

| 20% | 30% | 40% | 50% | 60% | 70% | 80% | 90% | 100% |

| 20% | 30% | 40% | 50% | 60% | 70% | 80% | 90% | 100% |

The choice of screen percentage is usually a matter of intuition. What are you trying to achieve with the type, and how legible must it be? Screens are traditionally specified in 5% increments, although computers enable you to input any percentage.

Working with process colors entails working with screens, for the wide ranging colors available for use are created with halftone dots of the process colors laid over one another (screen mixes). If type is printed in a combination of process screens – as it usually is – any inaccuracy in printing registration can result in soft, blurred, or ragged type due to straying dots. The problem is often compounded when both type and its background are printed with screen mixes. This problem is alleviated or eliminated when one or more of the process colors is 100%, when a high resolution halftone screen is used, when registration is accurate, and when type is not too small.

Type may safely be reversed from a four-color photograph to appear as white, or printed in color if there is enough contrast between the type and the photo. However, if type is too small or thin, there is an excellent chance the dots of the four-color image will invade the type characters and compromise their legibility (fig. **15**).

Outlines and shadows

If color contrast alone is not enough to make type stand out from its background, outlines and shadows can be useful. Since these treatments can be clumsy, trendy, and gimmicky, they should be used sparingly. Purpose and good judgment should guide their use. It is not advisable to use these effects with text type, for in terms of legibility they will do more harm than good. They are more successfully used with display type (fig. **16**).

A variety of outline and shadow effects.

16

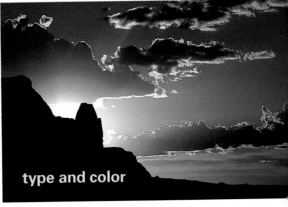

Compare the placement of type in this photograph. In the left example, it is difficult to read because of the competing background. The right example shows a much more effective positioning.

15

Working with color and type on the desktop

Know about color

Before you can get the most out of working with color and type, you should become completely familiar with the basic color and type topics presented in chapters 1-3 of this book. Seek other sources as well to gain as much knowledge as you can. But reading is only the first step; confidence and competence come only through dedicated, hands-on practice.

Define your objectives

What colors to add to type is never an arbitrary decision. Know your purpose and audience, and then choose color and type combinations that best represent them. With effective combinations of color and type, you can convey the intent of the message and set just the right mood. Always make typographic legibility your primary concern, departing from it only when appropriate.

Choose color for type and background

Remember that working with color and type is always a matter of both type *and* its background. You arrive at the most legible combinations when you strive for strong contrasts of hue (warm vs. cool), value (light vs. dark), saturation (vivid vs. dull), and combinations of these. But of these contrasts, value is the most critical. Think tints and shades before hues.

Choose dark on light combinations first

Type always reads better when letters are light and backgrounds are dark. But if light type on dark backgrounds works better for your purposes, go for it. Ultimately, the most important concept to remember is that contrast in value is essential.

Strive for color harmony

Though color harmony means many things to many people, a few suggestions will provide guidance: 1) Limit the number of colors to just a few, and select one to serve as the dominant color. 2) When considering hues, choose those with common characteristics such as analogous colors, or colors opposite one another on the color wheel. Harmony can result in both similar and dissimilar colors. 3) Don't use too many vivid colors; mix it up with shades and tints of well chosen pure hues. This will also provide your design with depth. 4) Use achromatic colors with pure hues, tints, and shades, as these combinations are always harmonious. 5) Begin with the basic color schemes shown on pages 26 and 27, and elaborate upon them as necessary.

Refer to color swatchbooks

When you are working on the computer desktop and you are selecting colors that will be printed, be aware that the computer screen does not accurately represent color. Always make color selections from printed swatchbooks, and then apply these selections to elements on the screen. You will then have an accurate idea about what the chosen colors will look like on press.

Select a color library

Whether working with spot or process (cmyk) color, choose a color-matching library and use it exclusively for each design job. Each library is based on a specific color system that will aid you in achieving consistency in your color selections. Color libraries include Pantone, Toyo, Trumatch, and Focoltone.

The color properties of hue, value, and saturation are important concerns when choosing color for type and its background. Carefully balancing these three color attributes leads to legible color and type combinations.

Color and type combinations

e color properties of hue, value, and saturation are criti-
l concerns when choosing color for type and its back-
ound. Carefully balancing these three color attributes
ads to legible color and type combinations. Color is an
pression of light on the computer screen, and because
its brightness and glow, it appears significantly different
an ink on paper. The combinations on the following
ges will aid you in making selections based upon the
pearance of color and type on the printed page. These
ecimens will also help you to assess the relative legi-
ity of color and type combinations and to venture into
ore daring and expressive color terrain. Though these
ecimens do not exhaust all color and type possibilities
o single source can), you will nonetheless find a practi-
l collection based upon an interaction of hues within
ve basic color schemes: primary, secondary, tertiary,
onochromatic, and achromatic. The color palette used is
esented on pages 20 and 21. It represents a thorough
nge of hues, values, and saturations. Each combination
numerically keyed to the process color conversion chart
page 154 for easy reference.

Since primary colors are equidistant on the color wheel, they offer significant hue contrasts. The primaries red and blue represent color temperature extremes. An interesting by-product of warm and cool colors is that warm colors appear to advance from the background, while cool colors recede. Make note of how the red type hovers above the blue backgrounds. Altering the saturation of the blue background aids legibility; compare the legibility of *1* and *5*.

color and type
color and **type**

1 | type **1** background **t41**

color and type
color and **type**

2 | type **1** background **t42**

color and type
color and **type**

3 | type **1** background **t43**

color and type
color and type

4 | type **1** background **t44**

color and type
color and **type**

5 | type **1** background **9**

color and type
color and **type**

6 | type **1** background **s41**

color and type
color and **type**

7 | type **1** background **s42**

color and type
color and **type**

8 | type **1** background **s43**

color and type
color and **type**

9 | type **1** background **s44**

color and type
color and **type**

10 | type **t1** background **9**

color and type
color and **type**

11 | type **t2** background **9**

color and type
color and **type**

12 | type **t3** background **9**

color and type
color and **type**

13 | type **t4** background **9**

color and type
color and **type**

14 | type **t5** background **9**

color and type
color and type

15 | type **s1** background **9**

color and type
color and type

16 | type **s2** background **9**

color and type
color and **type**

17 | type **s3** background **9**

color and type
color and **type**

18 | type **s4** background **9**

color and **type**

color and **type**

type **9** background **t1**

color and **type**

color and **type**

type **9** background **t2**

color and **type**

color and **type**

type **9** background **t3**

color and **type**

color and **type**

type **9** background **t4**

color and **type**

color and **type**

type **9** background **1**

color and **type**

color and **type**

type **9** background **s1**

color and type

color and type

type **9** background **s2**

color and type

color and type

type **9** background **s3**

color and type

color and type

type **9** background **s4**

28 | color and **type**

color and **type**

type **t41** background **1**

29 | color and type

color and **type**

type **t42** background **1**

30 | color and type

color and **type**

type **t43** background **1**

31 | color and type

color and type

type **t44** background **1**

32 | color and type

color and type

type **t45** background **1**

33 | color and **type**

color and **type**

type **s41** background **1**

34 | color and **type**

color and **type**

type **s42** background **1**

35 | color and **type**

color and **type**

type **s43** background **1**

36 | color and **type**

color and **type**

type **s44** background **1**

Because they are so vivid, the hot and saturated red backgrounds engulf blue type, making it difficult to read. Legibility improves immensely with lighter red backgrounds, but these backgrounds appear more pink than red (19-22).

Yellow is the most luminous of the primary colors. Shades of yellow cast a green tint, creating the illusion of a complementary color relationship (42-45). Darker shades of red appear burgundy, and provide a contrast to the yellow backgrounds that greatly enhances legibility (51-54).

color and **type**

color and **type**

37 | type **1** background **t21**

color and **type**

color and **type**

38 | type **1** background **t22**

color and **type**

color and **type**

39 | type **1** background **t23**

color and **type**

color and **type**

40 | type **1** background **t24**

color and **type**

color and **type**

41 | type **1** background **5**

color and **type**

color and **type**

42 | type **1** background **s21**

color and **type**

color and **type**

43 | type **1** background **s22**

color and **type**

color and type

44 | type **1** background **s23**

color and **type**

color and **type**

45 | type **1** background **s24**

color and type

color and type

46 | type **t1** background **5**

color and type

color and type

47 | type **t2** background **5**

color and **type**

color and type

48 | type **t3** background **5**

color and **type**

color and type

49 | type **t4** background **5**

color and **type**

color and **type**

50 | type **t5** background **5**

color and **type**

color and **type**

51 | type **s1** background **5**

color and **type**

color and **type**

52 | type **s2** background **5**

color and **type**

color and **type**

53 | type **s3** background **5**

color and **type**

color and **type**

54 | type **s4** background **5**

color and type

color and **type**

type **5** background **t1**

---

color and type

color and **type**

type **5** background **t2**

---

color and **type**

color and **type**

type **5** background **t3**

---

color and **type**

color and **type**

type **5** background **t4**

---

color and **type**

color and **type**

type **5** background **1**

---

color and **type**

color and **type**

type **5** background **s1**

---

color and **type**

color and **type**

type **5** background **s2**

---

color and **type**

color and **type**

type **5** background **s3**

---

color and **type**

color and **type**

type **5** background **s4**

---

color and **type**

color and **type**

64 | type **t21** background **1**

---

color and **type**

color and **type**

65 | type **t22** background **1**

---

color and **type**

color and **type**

66 | type **t23** background **1**

---

color and **type**

color and **type**

67 | type **t24** background **1**

---

color and **type**

color and **type**

68 | type **t25** background **1**

---

color and **type**

color and **type**

69 | type **s21** background **1**

---

color and **type**

color and **type**

70 | type **s22** background **1**

---

color and type

color and type

71 | type **s23** background **1**

---

color and **type**

color and **type**

72 | type **s24** background **1**

Yellow type on a light red background appears jaundiced and difficult to read (55), while on darker shades of red, it is much more legible (60-63). The fully saturated combination of red and yellow also produces satisfying results since the two hues already differ greatly in value (59).

The inherent value contrast of the pure hues yellow and blue provides excellent legibility (77). Blue type on tints of the yellow background (73-76) and shades of blue type on yellow backgrounds (87-90) further improve legibility. Darker shades of yellow begin to approximate the value of the blue type, leading to a reduction in legibility (79-81).

color and **type**

color and **type**

73 | type **9** background **t21**

color and **type**

color and **type**

74 | type **9** background **t22**

color and **type**

color and **type**

75 | type **9** background **t23**

color and **type**

color and **type**

76 | type **9** background **t24**

color and **type**

color and **type**

77 | type **9** background **5**

color and **type**

color and **type**

78 | type **9** background **s21**

color and **type**

color and **type**

79 | type **9** background **s22**

color and **type**

color and **type**

80 | type **9** background **s23**

81 | type **9** background **s24**

color and type

color and type

82 | type **t41** background **5**

color and type

color and type

83 | type **t42** background **5**

color and **type**

color and **type**

84 | type **t43** background **5**

color and **type**

color and **type**

85 | type **t44** background **5**

color and **type**

color and **type**

86 | type **t45** background **5**

color and **type**

color and **type**

87 | type **s41** background **5**

color and **type**

color and **type**

88 | type **s42** background **5**

color and **type**

color and **type**

89 | type **s43** background **5**

color and **type**

color and **type**

90 | type **s44** background **5**

color and type
color and type
type **5** background **t41**

color and **type**
color and **type**
100 type **t21** background **9**

color and **type**
color and **type**
type **5** background **t42**

color and **type**
color and **type**
101 type **t22** background **9**

color and **type**
color and **type**
type **5** background **t43**

color and **type**
color and **type**
102 type **t23** background **9**

color and **type**
color and **type**
type **5** background **t44**

color and **type**
color and **type**
103 type **t24** background **9**

color and **type**
color and **type**
type **5** background **9**

color and **type**
color and **type**
104 type **t25** background **9**

color and **type**
color and **type**
type **5** background **s41**

color and **type**
color and **type**
105 type **s21** background **9**

color and **type**
color and **type**
type **5** background **s42**

color and **type**
color and **type**
106 type **s22** background **9**

color and **type**
color and **type**
type **5** background **s43**

color and type
color and type
107 type **s23** background **9**

color and **type**
color and **type**
type **5** background **s44**

color and type
color and type
108 type **s24** background **9**

Placing yellow type on a blue background can be a very effective color combination, though overall, this combination is harder to read than the reverse. Yellow type on darker shades of blue (96-99) or tints of yellow on saturated blue backgrounds (100-104) provide acceptable legibility.

color and **type**

color and **type**

109 type **3** background **t31**

color and **type**

color and **type**

118 type **t11** background **7**

color and **type**

color and **type**

110 type **3** background **t32**

color and **type**

color and **type**

119 type **t12** background **7**

color and type

color and type

111 type **3** background **t33**

color and **type**

color and **type**

120 type **t13** background **7**

color and type

color and type

112 type **3** background **t34**

color and **type**

color and **type**

121 type **t14** background **7**

Because they are similar in value, the fully saturated secondary hues green and orange are not distinctive enough for a legible palette (113). Orange type on a light green background (109) appears more legible than orange type on a dark green background (117).

color and **type**

color and **type**

113 type **3** background **7**

color and **type**

color and **type**

122 type **t15** background **7**

color and **type**

color and **type**

114 type **3** background **s31**

color and type

color and type

123 type **s11** background **7**

color and **type**

color and **type**

115 type **3** background **s32**

color and type

color and type

124 type **s12** background **7**

color and **type**

color and **type**

116 type **3** background **s33**

color and **type**

color and **type**

125 type **s13** background **7**

color and **type**

color and **type**

117 type **3** background **s34**

color and **type**

color and **type**

126 type **s14** background **7**

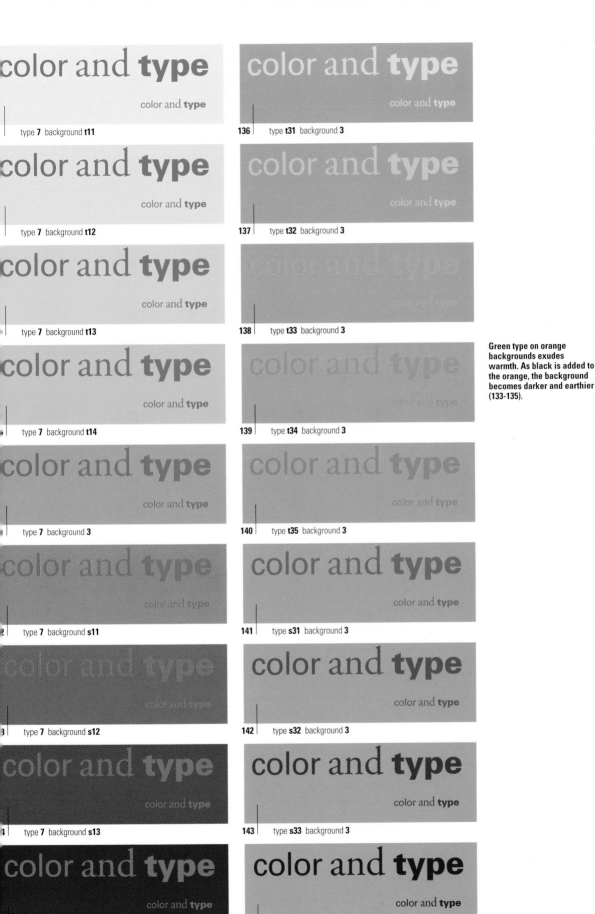

color and type

color and **type**

type **7** background **t11**

color and type

color and **type**

type **7** background **t12**

color and type

color and **type**

type **7** background **t13**

color and type

color and **type**

type **7** background **t14**

color and type

color and **type**

type **7** background **3**

color and type

color and **type**

type **7** background **s11**

color and type

color and type

type **7** background **s12**

color and type

color and **type**

type **7** background **s13**

color and type

color and **type**

type **7** background **s14**

color and type

color and **type**

136 type **t31** background **3**

color and type

color and **type**

137 type **t32** background **3**

color and type

color and type

138 type **t33** background **3**

color and type

color and type

139 type **t34** background **3**

color and type

color and type

140 type **t35** background **3**

color and type

color and **type**

141 type **s31** background **3**

color and type

color and **type**

142 type **s32** background **3**

color and type

color and **type**

143 type **s33** background **3**

color and type

color and **type**

144 type **s34** background **3**

Green type on orange backgrounds exudes warmth. As black is added to the orange, the background becomes darker and earthier (133-135).

Sufficient contrast between orange and violet translates into a readable color combination (149). As the shades of violet become darker, the orange type becomes more luminescent (150-153). The least readable combinations shown here are *147* and *162*. Violet is a regal color – pompous, sophisticated, and serious.

color and type color and type	**color and type** color and type
145 type **3** background **t51**	154 type **t11** background **11**
color and type color and type	**color and type** color and type
146 type **3** background **t52**	155 type **t12** background **11**
color and type color and type	**color and type** color and type
147 type **3** background **t53**	156 type **t13** background **11**
color and type color and type	**color and type** color and type
148 type **3** background **t54**	157 type **t14** background **11**
color and type color and type	**color and type** color and type
149 type **3** background **11**	158 type **t15** background **11**
color and type color and type	**color and type** color and type
150 type **3** background **s51**	159 type **s11** background **11**
color and type color and type	**color and type** color and type
151 type **3** background **s52**	160 type **s12** background **11**
color and type color and type	**color and type** color and type
152 type **3** background **s53**	161 type **s13** background **11**
color and type color and type	**color and type** color and type
153 type **3** background **s54**	162 type **s14** background **11**

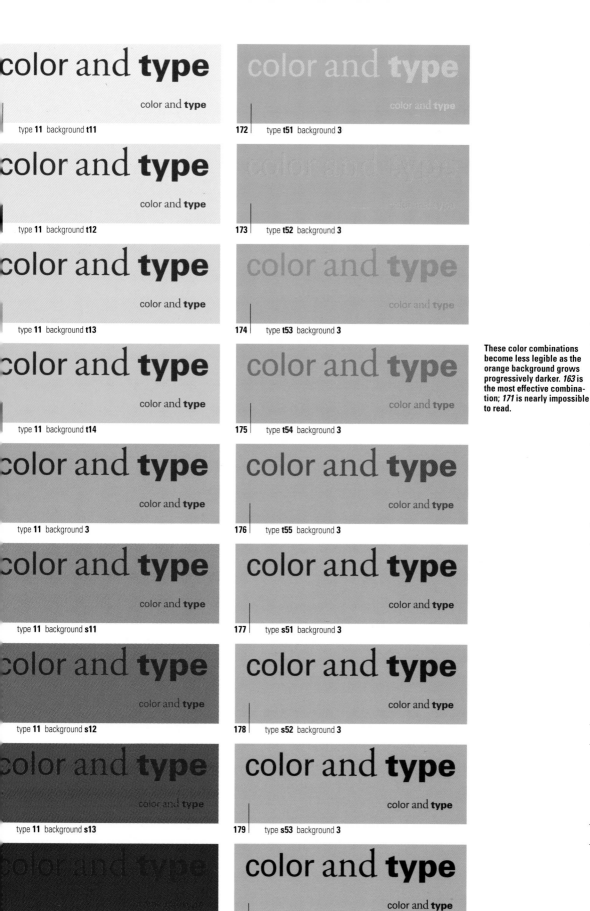

color and type

color and **type**

type **11** background **t11**

color and type

color and **type**

type **11** background **t12**

color and type

color and **type**

type **11** background **t13**

color and type

color and **type**

type **11** background **t14**

color and type

color and **type**

type **11** background **3**

color and type

color and **type**

type **11** background **s11**

color and type

color and **type**

type **11** background **s12**

color and type

color and **type**

type **11** background **s13**

color and type

type **11** background **s14**

172 type **t51** background **3**

color and **type**

color and **type**

173 type **t52** background **3**

174 type **t53** background **3**

color and **type**

color and **type**

175 type **t54** background **3**

color and **type**

color and **type**

176 type **t55** background **3**

color and **type**

color and **type**

177 type **s51** background **3**

color and **type**

color and **type**

178 type **s52** background **3**

color and **type**

color and **type**

179 type **s53** background **3**

color and **type**

color and **type**

180 type **s54** background **3**

These color combinations become less legible as the orange background grows progressively darker. *163* is the most effective combination; *171* is nearly impossible to read.

The fully saturated hues of green and violet offer enough contrast for reasonable legibility (185). Most difficult to read are *183* and *198,* where value and intensity are almost identical.

color and **type**

color and **type**

181 | type **7** background **t51**

color and **type**

color and **type**

182 | type **7** background **t52**

color and type

color and type

183 | type **7** background **t53**

color and type

color and type

184 | type **7** background **t54**

color and **type**

color and **type**

185 | type **7** background **11**

color and **type**

color and **type**

186 | type **7** background **s51**

color and **type**

color and **type**

187 | type **7** background **s52**

color and **type**

color and **type**

188 | type **7** background **s53**

color and **type**

color and **type**

189 | type **7** background **s54**

color and **type**

color and **type**

190 | type **t31** background **11**

color and **type**

color and **type**

191 | type **t32** background **11**

color and **type**

color and **type**

192 | type **t33** background **11**

color and **type**

color and **type**

193 | type **t34** background **11**

color and **type**

color and **type**

194 | type **t35** background **11**

color and **type**

color and **type**

195 | type **s31** background **11**

color and type

color and type

196 | type **s32** background **11**

color and type

color and type

197 | type **s33** background **11**

color and type

color and type

198 | type **s34** background **11**

color and **type**

color and **type**

type **11** background **t31**

color and **type**

color and **type**

type **11** background **t32**

color and **type**

color and **type**

type **11** background **t33**

color and **type**

color and **type**

type **11** background **t34**

color and **type**

color and **type**

type **11** background **7**

color and **type**

color and **type**

type **11** background **s31**

color and **type**

color and **type**

type **11** background **s32**

color and **type**

color and type

type **11** background **s33**

color and type

color and type

type **11** background **s34**

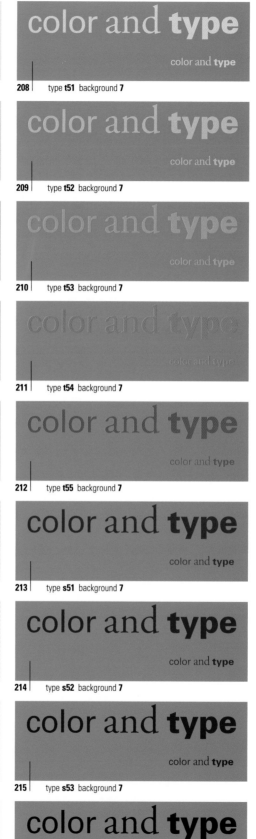

208 | color and **type** — color and **type** — type **t51** background **7**

209 | color and **type** — color and **type** — type **t52** background **7**

210 | color and type — color and type — type **t53** background **7**

211 | color and type — color and type — type **t54** background **7**

212 | color and **type** — color and **type** — type **t55** background **7**

213 | color and **type** — color and **type** — type **s51** background **7**

214 | color and **type** — color and **type** — type **s52** background **7**

215 | color and **type** — color and **type** — type **s53** background **7**

216 | color and **type** — color and **type** — type **s54** background **7**

Because saturated violet is a rather dark hue, type printed in this color on darker shades of green struggles for readability (204-207). The violet type is highly legible on lighter tints of green (199-202), as are shades of violet on green (213-216).

The two tertiary hues red-orange and yellow-orange lie close to one another on the color wheel. Since they are so similar, the most effective way to create sufficient contrast for type and background is through value. The red-orange type in full saturation reads best on lighter tints of yellow-orange (217-220); darker shades of red-orange type on yellow-orange backgrounds are also quite easy to negotiate with the eye (232-234). *223, 228, and 229* are nearly impossible to read.

color and type

color and **type**

217   type **2**   background **t16**

color and type

color and **type**

218   type **2**   background **t17**

color and type

color and **type**

219   type **2**   background **t18**

color and type

color and **type**

220   type **2**   background **t19**

color and type

color and **type**

221   type **2**   background **4**

color and type

color and **type**

222   type **2**   background **s16**

color and type

color and **type**

223   type **2**   background **s17**

color and type

color and **type**

224   type **2**   background **s18**

color and type

color and **type**

225   type **2**   background **s19**

color and type

color and **type**

226   type **t6**   background **4**

color and type

color and **type**

227   type **t7**   background **4**

color and type

color and **type**

228   type **t8**   background **4**

229   type **t9**   background **4**

color and type

color and **type**

230   type **t10**   background **4**

color and type

color and **type**

231   type **s6**   background **4**

color and type

color and **type**

232   type **s7**   background **4**

color and type

color and **type**

233   type **s8**   background **4**

color and type

color and **type**

234   type **s9**   background **4**

type **4** background **t6** 244 | type **t16** background **2**

type **4** background **t7** 245 | type **t17** background **2**

type **4** background **t8** 246 | type **t18** background **2**

type **4** background **t9** 247 | type **t19** background **2**

type **4** background **2** 248 | type **t20** background **2**

type **4** background **s6** 249 | type **s16** background **2**

type **4** background **s7** 250 | type **s17** background **2**

type **4** background **s8** 251 | type **s18** background **2**

type **4** background **s9** 252 | type **s19** background **2**

In reverse, this color combination lends better legibility with yellow-orange type placed on dark shades of the red-orange background (241-243), or with tints of yellow-orange type placed on red-orange backgrounds (244-246). These warm combinations are energetic and spontaneous.

Dissimilar hues are three colors apart on the color wheel. These combinations can appear quite harmonious and readable. Red-orange type on tints of yellow-green are highly readable (253-256), as are dark shades of yellow-orange type on yellow-green backgrounds (269, 270). On a somber, dark shade of yellow-green, the red-orange type reveals a glowing phosphorescence (261).

color and **type**

color and **type**

253 | type **2** background **t26**

color and **type**

color and **type**

254 | type **2** background **t27**

color and **type**

color and **type**

255 | type **2** background **t28**

color and **type**

color and **type**

256 | type **2** background **t29**

color and **type**

color and **type**

257 | type **2** background **6**

color and type

color and type

258 | type **2** background **s26**

color and **type**

color and type

259 | type **2** background **s27**

color and **type**

color and type

260 | type **2** background **s28**

color and **type**

color and **type**

261 | type **2** background **s29**

color and **type**

color and **type**

262 | type **t6** background **6**

color and **type**

color and **type**

263 | type **t7** background **6**

color and type

color and type

264 | type **t8** background **6**

color and type

color and type

265 | type **t9** background **6**

color and type

color and type

266 | type **t10** background **6**

color and **type**

color and type

267 | type **s6** background **6**

color and **type**

color and **type**

268 | type **s7** background **6**

color and **type**

color and **type**

269 | type **s8** background **6**

color and **type**

color and **type**

270 | type **s9** background **6**

type **6** background **t6**

280 type **t26** background **2**

type **6** background **t7**

281 type **t27** background **2**

type **6** background **t8**

282 type **t28** background **2**

type **6** background **t9**

283 type **t29** background **2**

type **6** background **2**

284 type **t30** background **2**

type **6** background **s6**

285 type **s26** background **2**

type **6** background **s7**

286 type **s27** background **2**

type **6** background **s8**

287 type **s28** background **2**

type **6** background **s9**

288 type **s29** background **2**

Placing yellow-green type on tints of red-orange is soft and tranquil (271-273). Light tints of yellow-green on red-orange prove quite legible (280-282), as well as yellow-green type on dark shades of red-orange (278-279).

Blue-green and red-orange are complementary colors, and when used at full saturation for type and background, the two colors vibrate and vie for attention (293). However, using red-orange type with turquoise (any of the lighter tints of blue-green) creates a harmonious, serene, and legible color combination (289-292). Straight red-orange type placed on darker shades of blue-green advances dynamically forward in space to create acceptable combinations (296, 297).

color and **type** color and **type** 289 | type **2** background **t36**	color and **type** color and **type** 298 | type **t6** background **8**
color and **type** color and **type** 290 | type **2** background **t37**	color and **type** color and **type** 299 | type **t7** background **8**
color and type color and **type** 291 | type **2** background **t38**	color and **type** color and **type** 300 | type **t8** background **8**
color and type color and type 292 | type **2** background **t39**	color and **type** color and **type** 301 | type **t9** background **8**
color and **type** color and **type** 293 | type **2** background **8**	color and **type** color and **type** 302 | type **t10** background **8**
color and **type** color and **type** 294 | type **2** background **s36**	color and type color and type 303 | type **s6** background **8**
color and **type** color and **type** 295 | type **2** background **s37**	color and type color and **type** 304 | type **s7** background **8**
color and **type** color and **type** 296 | type **2** background **s38**	color and **type** color and **type** 305 | type **s8** background **8**
color and **type** color and **type** 297 | type **2** background **s39**	color and **type** color and **type** 306 | type **s9** background **8**

type **8** background **t6**

type **8** background **t7**

type **8** background **t8**

type **8** background **t9**

type **8** background **2**

type **8** background **s6**

type **8** background **s7**

type **8** background **s8**

type **8** background **s9**

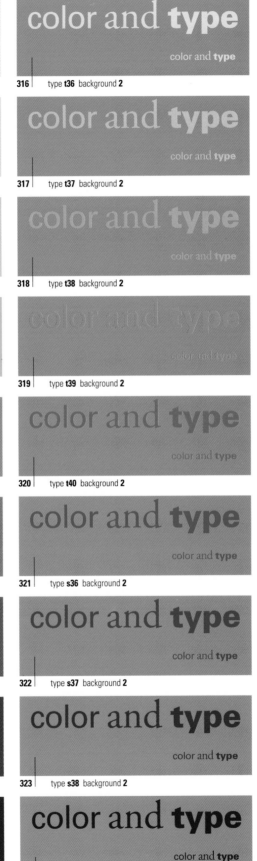

316 type **t36** background **2**

317 type **t37** background **2**

318 type **t38** background **2**

319 type **t39** background **2**

320 type **t40** background **2**

321 type **s36** background **2**

322 type **s37** background **2**

323 type **s38** background **2**

324 type **s39** background **2**

The simultaneous contrast effect (see chapter 2) is more pronounced when blue-green type is placed upon a red-orange background (311). This combination is best avoided unless you are seeking this vibrant effect. Using combinations of lighter tints and darker shades of these hues will encourage the reader to continue reading.

Red-orange and blue-violet produce a friendly, kinetic color combination. However, setting large amounts of type in this manner inhibits the reading process. Using this combination for display type can yield fresh and exciting results.

color and type
color and type
325   type **2**   background **t46**

color and type
color and type
326   type **2**   background **t47**

color and type
color and type
327   type **2**   background **t48**

color and type
color and type
328   type **2**   background **t49**

color and type
color and type
329   type **2**   background **10**

color and type
color and type
330   type **2**   background **s46**

color and type
color and type
331   type **2**   background **s47**

color and type
color and type
332   type **2**   background **s48**

color and type
color and type
333   type **2**   background **s49**

color and type
color and type
334   type **t6**   background **10**

color and type
color and type
335   type **t7**   background **10**

color and type
color and type
336   type **t8**   background **10**

color and type
color and type
337   type **t9**   background **10**

color and type
color and type
338   type **t10**   background **10**

color and type
color and type
339   type **s6**   background **10**

color and type
color and type
340   type **s7**   background **10**

color and type
color and type
341   type **s8**   background **10**

color and type
color and type
342   type **s9**   background **10**

color and type

color and **type**

type **10** background **t6**

color and type

color and **type**

type **10** background **t7**

color and type

color and **type**

type **10** background **t8**

color and type

color and **type**

type **10** background **t9**

color and type

color and **type**

type **10** background **2**

color and type

color and **type**

type **10** background **s6**

color and type

color and **type**

type **10** background **s7**

color and type

color and **type**

type **10** background **s8**

color and type

color and type

type **10** background **s9**

352 type **t46** background **2**

color and **type**

color and **type**

353 type **t47** background **2**

color and type

color and type

354 type **t48** background **2**

color and type

color and type

355 type **t49** background **2**

color and **type**

color and **type**

356 type **t50** background **2**

color and **type**

color and **type**

357 type **s46** background **2**

color and **type**

color and **type**

358 type **s47** background **2**

color and **type**

color and **type**

359 type **s48** background **2**

color and **type**

color and **type**

360 type **s49** background **2**

The simmering red-orange background is softened by the use of blue-violet for the type. Due to the relative darkness of blue-violet, legibility is compromised with the use of darker background shades of red-orange (349-351).

Neighbors on the color wheel, red-orange and red-violet have much in common. Combining them produces harmonious results, but because these hues are similar in value, it is advisable to use contrasting tints and shades. Compare the legibility of *361* with *365*.

color and type
color and type

361 | type **2** background **t56**

color and type
color and type

362 | type **2** background **t57**

color and type
color and type

363 | type **2** background **t58**

color and type
color and type

364 | type **2** background **t59**

color and type
color and type

365 | type **2** background **12**

color and type
color and type

366 | type **2** background **s56**

color and type
color and type

367 | type **2** background **s57**

color and type
color and type

368 | type **2** background **s58**

color and type
color and type

369 | type **2** background **s59**

color and **type**
color and **type**

370 | type **t6** background **12**

color and **type**
color and **type**

371 | type **t7** background **12**

color and **type**
color and **type**

372 | type **t8** background **12**

color and **type**
color and **type**

373 | type **t9** background **12**

color and **type**
color and **type**

374 | type **t10** background **12**

color and **type**
color and type

375 | type **s6** background **12**

color and type
color and type

376 | type **s7** background **12**

color and type
color and type

377 | type **s8** background **12**

color and type
color and type

378 | type **s9** background **12**

Each swatch reads "color and type / color and type".

type **12** background **t6**

type **12** background **t7**

type **12** background **t8**

type **12** background **t9**

type **12** background **2**

type **12** background **s6**

type **12** background **s7**

type **12** background **s8**

type **12** background **s9**

388 | type **t56** background **2**

389 | type **t57** background **2**

390 | type **t58** background **2**

391 | type **t59** background **2**

392 | type **t60** background **2**

393 | type **s56** background **2**

394 | type **s57** background **2**

395 | type **s58** background **2**

396 | type **s59** background **2**

Notice how the value of red-violet and the shade of red-orange in *385* and *391* are nearly identical. For optimum legibility, it is far better to select a background that differs more significantly in value, such as *379-381*. Of course, the appearance of a more legible color combination may not offer the desired color effect. Balancing the needs of legibility and color effect is always a challenging undertaking that necessitates careful consideration.

Yellow-orange and yellow-green are both light in value and very intense (401). It is best to combine extreme tints and shades as in *397, 405, 406,* and *414* for acceptable legibility. The yellow-green, which is accented with yellow-orange type, possesses a warmth and freshness that might remind you of a balmy summer day.

	color and type
397	type **4** background **t26**
398	type **4** background **t27**
399	type **4** background **t28**
400	type **4** background **t29**
401	type **4** background **6**
402	type **4** background **s26**
403	type **4** background **s27**
404	type **4** background **s28**
405	type **4** background **s29**
406	type **t16** background **6**
407	type **t17** background **6**
408	type **t18** background **6**
409	type **t19** background **6**
410	type **t20** background **6**
411	type **s16** background **6**
412	type **s17** background **6**
413	type **s18** background **6**
414	type **s19** background **6**

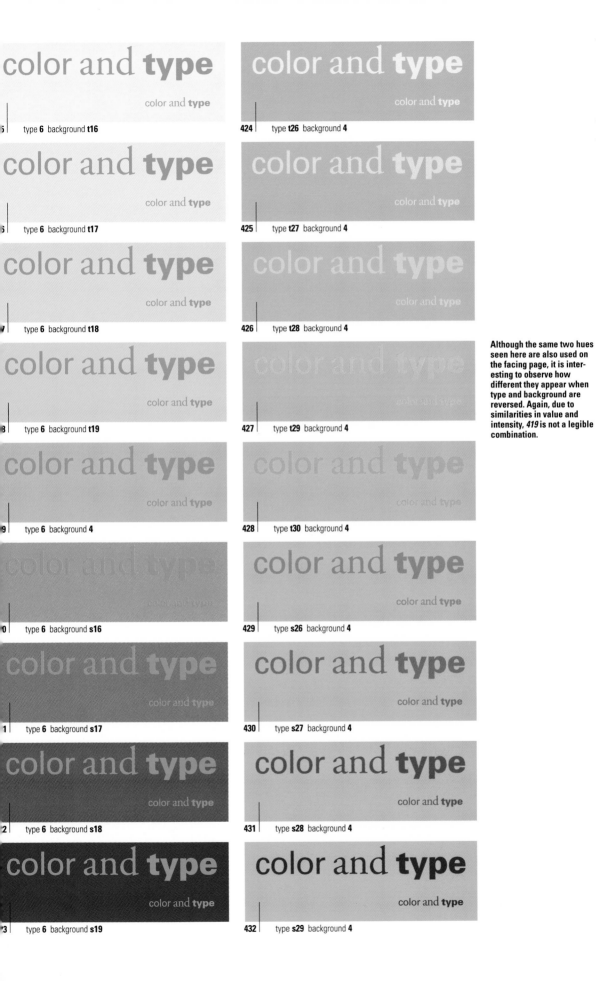

type **6** background **t16**

424 | type **t26** background **4**

type **6** background **t17**

425 | type **t27** background **4**

type **6** background **t18**

426 | type **t28** background **4**

type **6** background **t19**

427 | type **t29** background **4**

type **6** background **4**

428 | type **t30** background **4**

type **6** background **s16**

429 | type **s26** background **4**

type **6** background **s17**

430 | type **s27** background **4**

type **6** background **s18**

431 | type **s28** background **4**

type **6** background **s19**

432 | type **s29** background **4**

Although the same two hues seen here are also used on the facing page, it is interesting to observe how different they appear when type and background are reversed. Again, due to similarities in value and intensity, *419* is not a legible combination.

The yellow-orange type warms the cool, aquatic blue-green and they form a harmonious color alliance. The golden hue of the type provides enough body and strength to be quite readable when placed upon lighter tints of the background (433, 434). Placed upon darker shades of the background, the type casts an elegant glow (441).

433 type **4** background **t36**

434 type **4** background **t37**

435 type **4** background **t38**

436 type **4** background **t39**

437 type **4** background **8**

438 type **4** background **s36**

439 type **4** background **s37**

440 type **4** background **s38**

441 type **4** background **s39**

442 type **t16** background **8**

443 type **t17** background **8**

444 type **t18** background **8**

445 type **t19** background **8**

446 type **t20** background **8**

447 type **s16** background **8**

448 type **s17** background **8**

449 type **s18** background **8**

450 type **s19** background **8**

color and **type**

color and **type**

type **8** background **t16**

color and **type**

color and **type**

type **8** background **t17**

color and **type**

color and **type**

type **8** background **t18**

color and **type**

color and **type**

type **8** background **t19**

color and **type**

color and **type**

type **8** background **4**

color and **type**

color and **type**

type **8** background **s16**

color and **type**

color and **type**

type **8** background **s17**

color and **type**

color and **type**

type **8** background **s18**

color and **type**

color and **type**

type **8** background **s19**

color and **type**

color and **type**

460 type **t36** background **4**

color and **type**

color and **type**

461 type **t37** background **4**

color and **type**

color and **type**

462 type **t38** background **4**

color and **type**

color and **type**

463 type **t39** background **4**

color and **type**

color and **type**

464 type **t40** background **4**

color and **type**

color and **type**

465 type **s36** background **4**

color and **type**

color and **type**

466 type **s37** background **4**

color and **type**

color and **type**

467 type **s38** background **4**

color and **type**

color and **type**

468 type **s39** background **4**

Shades of yellow-orange are rich, warm, and earthy (458, 459). Adding blue-green type cools the palette, much as a stream brings relief to the heat of a desert. Obviously, *456, 457,462,* and *463* do not provide enough contrast between type and back-ground for sound legibility.

469 type **4** background **t46**

470 type **4** background **t47**

471 type **4** background **t48**

This color combination, a union of the complementary colors blue-violet and yellow-orange, connotes royalty, lavishness, and pomp and ceremony. Yellow-orange type stands out best and is most easy to read on darker shades of blue-violet (474-477).

472 type **4** background **t49**

473 type **4** background **10**

474 type **4** background **s46**

475 type **4** background **s47**

476 type **4** background **s48**

477 type **4** background **s49**

478 type **t16** background **10**

479 type **t17** background **10**

480 type **t18** background **10**

481 type **t19** background **10**

482 type **20** background **10**

483 type **s16** background **10**

484 type **s17** background **10**

485 type **s18** background **10**

486 type **s19** background **10**

color and type

color and **type**

type **10** background **t16**

---

color and type

color and **type**

type **10** background **t17**

---

color and type

color and **type**

type **10** background **t18**

---

color and type

color and **type**

type **10** background **t19**

---

color and type

color and **type**

type **10** background **4**

---

color and type

color and **type**

type **10** background **s16**

---

color and type

color and **type**

type **10** background **s17**

---

color and type

color and **type**

type **10** background **s18**

---

color and type

color and **type**

type **10** background **s19**

---

color and type

color and type

496 type **t46** background **4**

---

color and type

color and **type**

497 type **t47** background **4**

---

color and type

color and **type**

498 type **t48** background **4**

---

color and type

color and **type**

499 type **t49** background **4**

---

color and type

color and **type**

500 type **t50** background **4**

---

color and type

color and **type**

501 type **s46** background **4**

---

color and type

color and **type**

502 type **s47** background **4**

---

color and type

color and **type**

503 type **s48** background **4**

---

color and type

color and **type**

504 type **s49** background **4**

The inverse is true when yellow-orange type appears on blue-violet backgrounds; the lighter backgrounds give definition to the blue-violet type, which is quite dark at full saturation (487-490).

Lavenders – the lighter tints of red-violet – are nostalgic and romantic hues. When used as a background for yellow-orange type, however, it is advantageous to use darker values of yellow-orange (not shown). Another way to maintain legibility is to use either darker values of red-violet for the background rather than lighter values (510-513), or lighter values of yellow-orange type on saturated red-violet (514-516).

color and type
color and type
505 type **4** background **t56**

color and type
color and type
506 type **4** background **t57**

color and type
color and type
507 type **4** background **t58**

color and type
color and type
508 type **4** background **t59**

color and type
color and type
509 type **4** background **12**

color and type
color and type
510 type **4** background **s56**

color and type
color and type
511 type **4** background **s57**

color and type
color and type
512 type **4** background **s58**

color and type
color and type
513 type **4** background **s59**

color and type
color and type
514 type **t16** background **12**

color and type
color and type
515 type **t17** background **12**

color and type
color and type
516 type **t18** background **12**

color and type
color and type
517 type **t19** background **12**

color and type
color and type
518 type **t20** background **12**

color and type
color and type
519 type **s16** background **12**

color and type
color and type
520 type **s17** background **12**

color and type
color and type
521 type **s18** background **12**

color and type
color and type
522 type **s19** background **12**

color and **type**

color and **type**

type **12** background **t16**

color and **type**

color and **type**

type **12** background **t17**

color and **type**

color and **type**

type **12** background **t18**

color and **type**

color and **type**

type **12** background **t19**

color and **type**

color and **type**

type **12** background **4**

color and **type**

color and **type**

type **12** background **s16**

color and **type**

color and **type**

type **12** background **s17**

color and **type**

color and **type**

type **12** background **s18**

color and **type**

color and **type**

type **12** background **s19**

532 | type **t56** background **4**

color and **type**

color and **type**

533 | type **t57** background **4**

color and **type**

color and **type**

534 | type **t58** background **4**

color and **type**

color and **type**

535 | type **t59** background **4**

color and **type**

color and **type**

536 | type **t60** background **4**

color and **type**

color and **type**

537 | type **s56** background **4**

color and **type**

color and **type**

538 | type **s57** background **4**

color and **type**

color and **type**

539 | type **s58** background **4**

color and **type**

color and **type**

540 | type **s59** background **4**

Using fully saturated red-violet type on a fully saturated yellow-orange background is quite legible due to the contrasting characteristics of these basic hues (527).

color and type

color and **type**

541 | type **6** background **t36**

color and type

color and **type**

542 | type **6** background **t37**

color and type

color and type

543 | type **6** background **t38**

color and type

color and type

544 | type **6** background **t39**

This analogous combination is mellow, cool, and refreshing. Compare *549, 550,* and *558,* which are acceptably legible, with the marginally legible *544, 555,* and *556.*

color and type

color and **type**

545 | type **6** background **8**

color and type

color and **type**

546 | type **6** background **s36**

color and type

color and **type**

547 | type **6** background **s37**

color and type

color and **type**

548 | type **6** background **s38**

color and type

color and **type**

549 | type **6** background **s39**

color and type

color and **type**

550 | type **t26** background **8**

color and type

color and **type**

551 | type **t27** background **8**

color and **type**

color and **type**

552 | type **t28** background **8**

color and **type**

color and type

553 | type **t29** background **8**

color and **type**

color and **type**

554 | type **t30** background **8**

color and type

color and type

555 | type **s26** background **8**

color and type

color and type

556 | type **s27** background **8**

color and **type**

color and **type**

557 | type **s28** background **8**

color and **type**

color and **type**

558 | type **s29** background **8**

color and **type**

color and **type**

type **8** background **t26**

color and **type**

color and **type**

type **8** background **t27**

color and **type**

color and **type**

type **8** background **t28**

color and **type**

color and **type**

type **8** background **t29**

color and **type**

color and **type**

type **8** background **6**

color and **type**

color and **type**

type **8** background **s26**

color and **type**

color and **type**

type **8** background **s27**

color and **type**

color and **type**

type **8** background **s28**

color and **type**

color and **type**

type **8** background **s29**

---

color and **type**

color and **type**

568 type **t36** background **6**

color and **type**

color and **type**

569 type **t37** background **6**

color and **type**

color and **type**

570 type **t38** background **6**

color and **type**

color and **type**

571 type **t39** background **6**

color and **type**

color and **type**

572 type **t30** background **6**

color and **type**

color and **type**

573 type **s36** background **6**

color and **type**

color and **type**

574 type **s37** background **6**

color and **type**

color and **type**

575 type **s38** background **6**

color and **type**

color and **type**

576 type **s39** background **6**

Among these lush combinations, *559* and *576* offer a high degree of legibility. Compare with *564, 565,* 570, and *571.*

It is interesting to note the wide variety of color effects that can be achieved with colors belonging to the same families of hue. Variations in value and saturation make this possible. Compare, for example, the startling differences between *577, 581,* and *585.* While the type's hue remains constant, a shift in the value and saturation of the backgrounds gives each a unique appearance.

color and **type**

color and **type**

577 | type **6** background **t46**

color and **type**

color and **type**

578 | type **6** background **t47**

color and **type**

color and **type**

579 | type **6** background **t48**

color and **type**

color and **type**

580 | type **6** background **t49**

color and **type**

color and **type**

581 | type **6** background **10**

color and **type**

color and **type**

582 | type **6** background **s46**

color and **type**

color and **type**

583 | type **6** background **s47**

color and **type**

color and **type**

584 | type **6** background **s48**

color and **type**

color and **type**

585 | type **6** background **s49**

color and **type**

color and **type**

586 | type **t26** background **10**

color and **type**

color and **type**

587 | type **t27** background **10**

color and **type**

color and **type**

588 | type **t28** background **10**

color and **type**

color and **type**

589 | type **t29** background **10**

color and **type**

color and **type**

590 | type **t30** background **10**

color and **type**

color and **type**

591 | type **s26** background **10**

color and **type**

color and **type**

592 | type **s27** background **10**

color and **type**

color and **type**

593 | type **s28** background **10**

color and **type**

color and **type**

594 | type **s29** background **10**

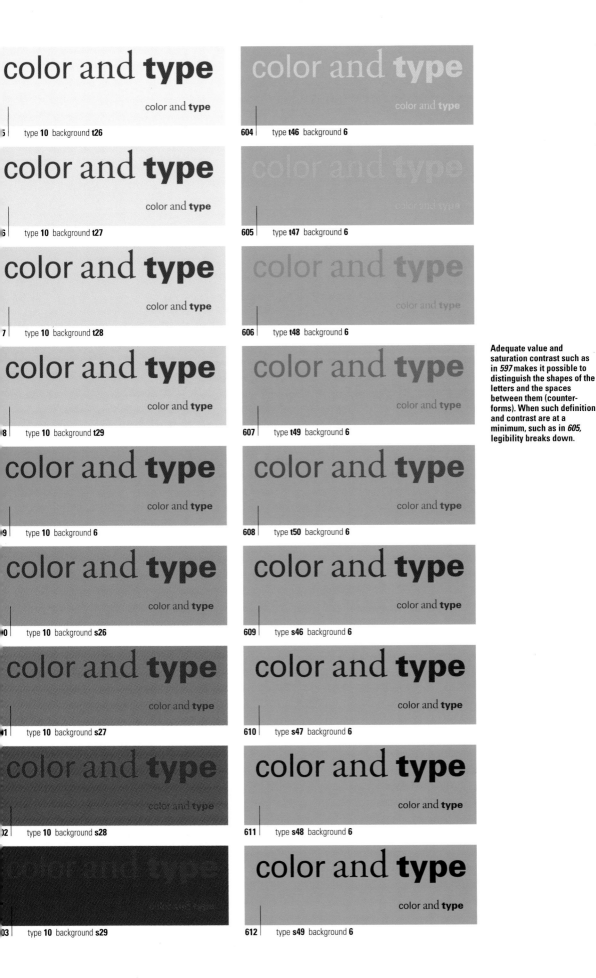

color and **type**

color and **type**

5 | type **10** background **t26**

604 | type **t46** background **6**

color and **type**

color and **type**

6 | type **10** background **t27**

605 | type **t47** background **6**

color and **type**

color and **type**

7 | type **10** background **t28**

606 | type **t48** background **6**

color and **type**

color and **type**

color and **type**

color and **type**

8 | type **10** background **t29**

607 | type **t49** background **6**

color and **type**

color and **type**

color and **type**

color and **type**

9 | type **10** background **6**

608 | type **t50** background **6**

color and **type**

color and **type**

color and **type**

color and **type**

0 | type **10** background **s26**

609 | type **s46** background **6**

color and **type**

color and **type**

color and **type**

color and **type**

1 | type **10** background **s27**

610 | type **s47** background **6**

color and **type**

color and **type**

color and **type**

color and **type**

02 | type **10** background **s28**

611 | type **s48** background **6**

color and type

color and **type**

color and **type**

03 | type **10** background **s29**

612 | type **s49** background **6**

Adequate value and saturation contrast such as in *597* makes it possible to distinguish the shapes of the letters and the spaces between them (counter-forms). When such definition and contrast are at a minimum, such as in *605*, legibility breaks down.

Combinations of the complementary hues red-violet and yellow-green are slightly off beat and whimsical. Darker shades of red-violet acquire an air of mystery and magic (620, 621).

color and type
color and type
613 | type **6** background **t56**

color and type
color and type
614 | type **6** background **t57**

color and type
color and type
615 | type **6** background **t58**

color and type
color and type
616 | type **6** background **t59**

color and type
color and type
617 | type **6** background **12**

color and type
color and type
618 | type **6** background **s56**

color and type
color and type
619 | type **6** background **s57**

color and type
color and type
620 | type **6** background **s58**

color and type
color and type
621 | type **6** background **s59**

color and type
color and type
622 | type **t26** background **12**

color and type
color and type
623 | type **t27** background **12**

color and type
color and type
624 | type **t28** background **12**

color and type
color and type
625 | type **t29** background **12**

color and type
color and type
626 | type **t30** background **12**

color and type
color and type
627 | type **s26** background **12**

color and type
color and type
628 | type **s27** background **12**

color and type
color and type
629 | type **s28** background **12**

color and type
color and type
630 | type **s29** background **12**

color and type

color and **type**

type **12** background **t26**

color and type

color and **type**

type **12** background **t27**

color and type

color and **type**

type **12** background **t28**

color and type

color and **type**

type **12** background **t29**

color and type

color and **type**

type **12** background **6**

color and type

color and **type**

type **12** background **s26**

color and type

color and **type**

type **12** background **s27**

color and **type**

color and **type**

type **12** background **s28**

color and type

color and type

type **12** background **s29**

640 | type **t56** background **6**

color and **type**

color and **type**

641 | type **t57** background **6**

color and type

color and type

642 | type **t58** background **6**

color and **type**

color and **type**

643 | type **t59** background **6**

color and type

color and **type**

644 | type **t60** background **6**

color and type

color and **type**

645 | type **s56** background **6**

color and **type**

color and **type**

646 | type **s57** background **6**

color and **type**

color and **type**

647 | type **s58** background **6**

color and **type**

color and **type**

648 | type **s59** background **6**

Lighter and more subtle tints of yellow-green lose the vivid impact of the pure hue. When used as backgrounds for red-violet type, however, legibility improves (631-634).

Tertiary

In partnership, blue-green and blue-violet appear calm and restful. These analogous hues remind us perhaps of a peaceful and tranquil sea. Plenty of value contrast is needed to ensure legibility when these colors are used for type and background. Compare *658* and *666*.

color and **type**

color and **type**

649 type **8** background **t46**

color and **type**

color and **type**

650 type **8** background **t47**

color and **type**

color and **type**

651 type **8** background **t48**

color and **type**

color and **type**

652 type **8** background **t49**

color and **type**

color and **type**

653 type **8** background **10**

color and **type**

color and **type**

654 type **8** background **s46**

color and **type**

color and **type**

655 type **8** background **s47**

color and **type**

color and **type**

656 type **8** background **s48**

color and **type**

color and **type**

657 type **8** background **s49**

color and **type**

color and **type**

658 type **t36** background **10**

color and **type**

color and **type**

659 type **t37** background **10**

color and **type**

color and **type**

660 type **t38** background **10**

color and **type**

color and **type**

661 type **t39** background **10**

color and **type**

color and **type**

662 type **t40** background **10**

color and **type**

color and **type**

663 type **s36** background **10**

color and **type**

color and **type**

664 type **s37** background **10**

color and **type**

color and **type**

665 type **s38** background **10**

color and **type**

color and **type**

666 type **s39** background **10**

color and **type**

color and **type**

type **10** background **t36**

color and **type**

color and **type**

type **10** background **t37**

color and **type**

color and **type**

type **10** background **t38**

color and **type**

color and **type**

type **10** background **t39**

color and **type**

color and **type**

type **10** background **8**

color and **type**

color and **type**

type **10** background **s36**

color and **type**

color and **type**

type **10** background **s37**

color and type

color and type

type **10** background **s38**

type **10** background **s39**

color and **type**

color and **type**

676 | type **t46** background **8**

color and **type**

color and **type**

677 | type **t47** background **8**

color and type

color and type

678 | type **t48** background **8**

color and type

color and type

679 | type **t49** background **8**

color and **type**

color and **type**

680 | type **t50** background **8**

color and **type**

color and **type**

681 | type **s46** background **8**

color and **type**

color and **type**

682 | type **s47** background **8**

color and **type**

color and **type**

683 | type **s48** background **8**

color and **type**

color and **type**

684 | type **s49** background **8**

By reversing the type-background relationship, the effect is subtly warmer. When considering color for type, consider the content. Though two colors may be quite similar, the slight differ-ence between them can have an enormous impact upon the typographic message.

Color temperature affects the relationship between these two hues in a most subtle way, for red-violet leans towards red and the warm side of the color wheel. Approaching green on the color wheel, blue-green is cool. Color temperature distinctions, regardless of their subtlety, are important to keep in mind when choosing colors.

color and **type**

color and **type**

685 | type **8** background **t56**

color and **type**

color and **type**

686 | type **8** background **t57**

color and **type**

color and **type**

687 | type **8** background **t58**

color and **type**

color and **type**

688 | type **8** background **t59**

color and **type**

color and **type**

689 | type **8** background **12**

color and **type**

color and **type**

690 | type **8** background **s56**

color and **type**

color and **type**

691 | type **8** background **s57**

color and **type**

color and **type**

692 | type **8** background **s58**

color and **type**

color and **type**

693 | type **8** background **s59**

color and **type**

color and **type**

694 | type **t36** background **12**

color and **type**

color and **type**

695 | type **t37** background **12**

color and **type**

color and **type**

696 | type **t38** background **12**

color and **type**

color and **type**

697 | type **t39** background **12**

color and **type**

color and **type**

698 | type **t40** background **12**

color and **type**

color and **type**

699 | type **s36** background **12**

color and **type**

color and **type**

700 | type **s37** background **12**

color and **type**

color and **type**

701 | type **s38** background **12**

color and **type**

color and **type**

702 | type **s39** background **12**

color and **type**

color and **type**

type **12** background **t36**

712 | type **t56** background **8**

color and **type**

color and **type**

type **12** background **t37**

713 | type **t57** background **8**

color and **type**

color and **type**

type **12** background **t38**

714 | type **t58** background **8**

color and **type**

color and **type**

type **12** background **t39**

715 | type **t59** background **8**

color and **type**

color and **type**

type **12** background **8**

716 | type **t60** background **8**

color and **type**

color and **type**

type **12** background **s36**

717 | type **s56** background **8**

color and **type**

color and **type**

type **12** background **s37**

718 | type **s57** background **8**

color and type

color and **type**

type **12** background **s38**

719 | type **s58** background **8**

color and **type**

color and **type**

type **12** background **s39**

720 | type **s59** background **8**

703-706 and 717-720 are the most legible as well as the safest combinations shown here. However, 711 offers a more dramatic possibility that might be appropriate for use with display type. Compare the legibility of the display type and the text type in this combination. When a color combination might be marginal, try enlarging the type for better results.

Tertiary

Blue-violet and red-violet are cousins on the color wheel, and they possess extraordinary richness. Fully saturated hues, such as *725,* are always more vivid than tints and shades. When white is added, such as in the background tints of *721-724,* the hues become softer and more pastelle in appearance.

color and **type**

color and **type**

721 | type **10** background **t56**

color and **type**

color and **type**

722 | type **10** background **t57**

color and **type**

color and **type**

723 | type **10** background **t58**

color and **type**

color and **type**

724 | type **10** background **t59**

725 | type **10** background **12**

726 | type **10** background **s56**

727 | type **10** background **s57**

728 | type **10** background **s58**

729 | type **10** background **s59**

color and **type**

color and **type**

730 | type **t46** background **12**

color and **type**

color and **type**

731 | type **t47** background **12**

732 | type **t48** background **12**

color and **type**

color and **type**

733 | type **t49** background **12**

734 | type **t50** background **12**

color and **type**

color and **type**

735 | type **s46** background **12**

color and **type**

color and **type**

736 | type **s47** background **12**

color and **type**

color and **type**

737 | type **s48** background **12**

color and **type**

color and **type**

738 | type **s49** background **12**

color and type

color and **type**

type **12** background **t46**

---

color and type

color and **type**

type **12** background **t47**

---

color and **type**

color and **type**

type **12** background **t48**

---

color and **type**

color and **type**

type **12** background **t49**

---

color and **type**

color and **type**

type **12** background **10**

---

color and **type**

color and **type**

type **12** background **s46**

---

color and **type**

color and **type**

type **12** background **s47**

---

color and **type**

color and **type**

type **12** background **s48**

---

color and **type**

color and **type**

type **12** background **s49**

---

color and type

color and **type**

748 | type **t56** background **10**

---

color and type

color and **type**

749 | type **t57** background **10**

---

color and **type**

color and **type**

750 | type **t58** background **10**

---

color and **type**

color and **type**

751 | type **t59** background **10**

---

color and **type**

color and **type**

752 | type **t60** background **10**

---

color and **type**

color and **type**

753 | type **s56** background **10**

---

color and type

color and type

754 | type **s57** background **10**

---

color and type

color and type

755 | type **s58** background **10**

---

color and **type**

color and **type**

756 | type **s59** background **10**

A color becomes duller as black or its complement is added to it (compare the type in *753-756*). If you wish to tone down vivid type, try adding black. If the type's background is dark, you may have to lighten it to preserve legibility.

When the same hue is used for both type and background, the only way to establish contrast is through value. As type and background approach the same value, legibility diminishes. Compare *757* with *761*.

color and type
color and **type**

757 | type **1** background **t1**

color and **type**
color and **type**

758 | type **1** background **t2**

color and **type**
color and **type**

759 | type **1** background **t3**

color and **type**
color and **type**

760 | type **1** background **t4**

color and **type**
color and **type**

761 | type **1** background **t5**

color and type
color and type

762 | type **1** background **s1**

color and type
color and **type**

763 | type **1** background **s2**

color and type
color and type

764 | type **1** background **s3**

color and **type**
color and **type**

765 | type **1** background **s4**

color and **type**
color and **type**

766 | type **t1** background **1**

color and **type**
color and **type**

767 | type **t2** background **1**

color and **type**
color and **type**

768 | type **t3** background **1**

color and **type**
color and **type**

769 | type **t4** background **1**

color and type
color and type

770 | type **t5** background **1**

color and type
color and type

771 | type **s1** background **1**

color and **type**
color and **type**

772 | type **s2** background **1**

color and **type**
color and type

773 | type **s3** background **1**

color and **type**
color and **type**

774 | type **s4** background **1**

color and type	**color and type**	
color and **type**	color and **type**	

color and type

color and **type**

color and **type**

color and **type**

color and **type**

color and **type**

color and **type**

color and **type**

color and **type**

color and **type**

color and **type**

color and **type**

color and **type**

color and **type**

color and **type**

color and **type**

color and **type**

color and **type**

color and **type**

color and **type**

color and type

color and **type**

type **9** background **t41**

784 | type **t41** background **9**

type **9** background **t42**

785 | type **t42** background **9**

type **9** background **t43**

786 | type **t43** background **9**

type **9** background **t44**

787 | type **t44** background **9**

type **9** background **t45**

788 | type **t45** background **9**

type **9** background **s41**

789 | type **s41** background **9**

type **9** background **s42**

790 | type **s42** background **9**

type **9** background **s43**

791 | type **s43** background **9**

type **9** background **s44**

792 | type **s44** background **9**

Even though you may be limited to the use of a single color, you can achieve a great deal of chromatic variety by juxtaposing different values of the color.

When working with type, the achromatic colors black, white, and gray are extremely useful. Because of their absolute neutrality, they are highly versatile. This is a no-nonsense palette: resolute, serious, and businesslike.

color and **type**

color and **type**

793 | type **k10** background **k1**

color and **type**

color and **type**

794 | type **k10** background **k2**

color and **type**

color and **type**

795 | type **k10** background **k3**

color and **type**

color and **type**

796 | type **k10** background **k4**

color and **type**

color and **type**

797 | type **k10** background **k5**

color and **type**

color and **type**

798 | type **k10** background **k6**

color and **type**

color and **type**

799 | type **k10** background **k7**

color and **type**

color and **type**

800 | type **k10** background **k8**

color and **type**

color and **type**

801 | type **k10** background **k9**

color and **type**

color and **type**

802 | type **k1** background **k10**

color and **type**

color and **type**

803 | type **k2** background **k10**

color and **type**

color and **type**

804 | type **k3** background **k10**

color and **type**

color and **type**

805 | type **k4** background **k10**

color and **type**

color and **type**

806 | type **k5** background **k10**

color and **type**

color and **type**

807 | type **k6** background **k10**

color and **type**

color and **type**

808 | type **k7** background **k10**

color and **type**

color and **type**

809 | type **k8** background **k10**

color and type

810 | type **k9** background **k10**

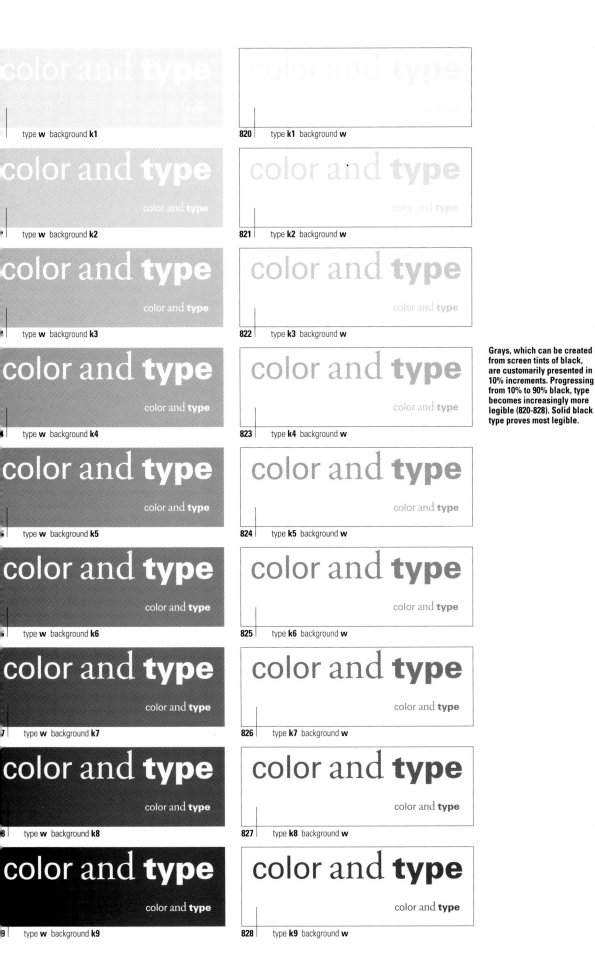

type **w** background **k1**

820 type **k1** background **w**

type **w** background **k2**

821 type **k2** background **w**

type **w** background **k3**

822 type **k3** background **w**

type **w** background **k4**

823 type **k4** background **w**

Grays, which can be created from screen tints of black, are customarily presented in 10% increments. Progressing from 10% to 90% black, type becomes increasingly more legible (820-828). Solid black type proves most legible.

type **w** background **k5**

824 type **k5** background **w**

type **w** background **k6**

825 type **k6** background **w**

type **w** background **k7**

826 type **k7** background **w**

type **w** background **k8**

827 type **k8** background **w**

type **w** background **k9**

828 type **k9** background **w**

The next six pages display type in the 12 basic hues of the color wheel on white, gray, and black backgrounds. You will find that each hue responds differently to the achromatic palette and that legibility differs enormously depending upon the value and intensity of each hue. Legibility is at its worst when the values of the background and the type become too similar. For example, the red type in *834* approximates the gray background, leading to a decrease in legibility.

color and **type**
color and **type**

829 | type **1** background **w**

color and **type**
color and **type**

830 | type **1** background **k2**

color and **type**
color and **type**

831 | type **1** background **k3**

color and **type**
color and **type**

832 | type **1** background **k4**

color and **type**
color and **type**

833 | type **1** background **k5**

color and **type**
color and **type**

834 | type **1** background **k6**

color and **type**
color and **type**

835 | type **1** background **k7**

color and **type**
color and **type**

836 | type **1** background **k8**

color and **type**
color and **type**

837 | type **1** background **k10**

color and **type**
color and **type**

838 | type **2** background **w**

color and **type**
color and **type**

839 | type **2** background **k2**

color and **type**
color and **type**

840 | type **2** background **k3**

color and **type**
color and **type**

841 | type **2** background **k4**

color and **type**
color and **type**

842 | type **2** background **k5**

color and **type**
color and **type**

843 | type **2** background **k6**

color and **type**
color and **type**

844 | type **2** background **k7**

color and **type**
color and **type**

845 | type **2** background **k8**

color and **type**
color and **type**

846 | type **2** background **k10**

color and **type**

color and **type**

type **3** background **w**

---

color and **type**

color and **type**

856 type **4** background **w**

---

color and **type**

color and **type**

type **3** background **k2**

---

color and **type**

color and **type**

857 type **4** background **k2**

---

color and **type**

color and **type**

type **3** background **k3**

---

color and **type**

color and **type**

858 type **4** background **k3**

---

color and **type**

color and **type**

type **3** background **k4**

---

color and **type**

color and **type**

859 type **4** background **k4**

---

color and **type**

color and **type**

type **3** background **k5**

---

color and **type**

color and **type**

860 type **4** background **k5**

---

color and **type**

color and **type**

type **3** background **k6**

---

color and **type**

color and **type**

861 type **4** background **k6**

---

color and **type**

color and **type**

type **3** background **k7**

---

color and **type**

color and **type**

862 type **4** background **k7**

---

color and **type**

color and **type**

type **3** background **k8**

---

color and **type**

color and **type**

863 type **4** background **k8**

---

color and **type**

color and **type**

5 type **3** background **k10**

---

color and **type**

color and **type**

864 type **4** background **k10**

Regardless of which hue is combined with white, black, or gray, the result is almost always harmonious and beautiful. The achromatic hues enhance the chromatic hues, never competing with their essential qualities.

On a white background, yellow type lacks definition (865). As backgrounds grow darker, type becomes more vivid (866-872). Too much contrast can also affect legibility. On black, for example, yellow type creates a dazzle that can tire a reader if used for large quantities of text type (873).

color and **type**

color and **type**

865 | type **5** background **w**

color and **type**

color and **type**

874 | type **6** background **w**

color and **type**

color and **type**

866 | type **5** background **k2**

color and **type**

color and **type**

875 | type **6** background **k2**

color and **type**

color and **type**

867 | type **5** background **k3**

color and **type**

color and **type**

876 | type **6** background **k3**

color and **type**

color and **type**

868 | type **5** background **k4**

color and **type**

color and type

877 | type **6** background **k4**

color and **type**

color and **type**

869 | type **5** background **k5**

color and type

color and type

878 | type **6** background **k5**

color and **type**

color and **type**

870 | type **5** background **k6**

color and **type**

color and **type**

879 | type **6** background **k6**

color and **type**

color and **type**

871 | type **5** background **k7**

color and **type**

color and **type**

880 | type **6** background **k7**

color and **type**

color and **type**

872 | type **5** background **k8**

color and **type**

color and **type**

881 | type **6** background **k8**

color and **type**

color and **type**

873 | type **5** background **k10**

color and **type**

color and **type**

882 | type **6** background **k10**

color and **type** # color and **type**

color and **type** color and **type**

color and **type** color and **type**

3 | type **7** background **w** 892 | type **8** background **w**

color and **type** color and **type**

color and **type** color and **type**

4 | type **7** background **k2** 893 | type **8** background **k2**

color and **type** color and **type**

color and **type** color and **type**

5 | type **7** background **k3** 894 | type **8** background **k3**

color and **type** color and **type**

color and **type** color and **type**

6 | type **7** background **k4** 895 | type **8** background **k4**

color and **type** color and **type**

color and type color and type

7 | type **7** background **k5** 896 | type **8** background **k5**

color and type color and type

color and type color and type

8 | type **7** background **k6** 897 | type **8** background **k6**

color and **type** color and **type**

color and type color and type

9 | type **7** background **k7** 898 | type **8** background **k7**

color and **type** color and **type**

color and **type** color and **type**

0 | type **7** background **k8** 899 | type **8** background **k8**

color and **type** color and **type**

color and **type** color and **type**

1 | type **7** background **k10** 900 | type **8** background **k10**

Type in each hue appears to change colors as it interacts differently with each achromatic background. Notice how the green and blue-green type nearly disappears on the 50% gray background (887, 896).

Blue type is peaceful and
soothing on gray. It reads
best on white and the lighter
shades of gray (901-904).
Legibility suffers on the
darker shades of gray and
black (905-909). This is
generally true of all of the
darker hues.

color and **type**

color and **type**

901 | type **9** background **w**

color and **type**

color and **type**

902 | type **9** background **k2**

color and **type**

color and **type**

903 | type **9** background **k3**

color and **type**

color and **type**

904 | type **9** background **k4**

color and **type**

color and **type**

905 | type **9** background **k5**

color and **type**

color and **type**

906 | type **9** background **k6**

color and **type**

color and **type**

907 | type **9** background **k7**

color and **type**

color and **type**

908 | type **9** background **k8**

color and **type**

color and **type**

909 | type **9** background **k10**

color and **type**

color and **type**

910 | type **10** background **w**

color and **type**

color and **type**

911 | type **10** background **k2**

color and **type**

color and **type**

912 | type **10** background **k3**

color and **type**

color and **type**

913 | type **10** background **k4**

color and **type**

color and **type**

914 | type **10** background **k5**

color and **type**

color and **type**

915 | type **10** background **k6**

color and **type**

color and **type**

916 | type **10** background **k7**

color and **type**

color and **type**

917 | type **10** background **k8**

color and **type**

color and **type**

918 | type **10** background **k10**

color and **type**

color and **type**

type **11** background **w**

color and **type**

color and **type**

type **11** background **k2**

color and **type**

color and **type**

type **11** background **k3**

color and **type**

color and **type**

type **11** background **k4**

color and **type**

color and **type**

type **11** background **k5**

color and **type**

color and **type**

type **11** background **k6**

color and **type**

color and **type**

type **11** background **k7**

color and **type**

color and **type**

type **11** background **k8**

color and **type**

color and type

type **11** background **k10**

color and **type**

color and **type**

928 | type **12** background **w**

color and **type**

color and **type**

929 | type **12** background **k2**

color and **type**

color and **type**

930 | type **12** background **k3**

color and **type**

color and **type**

931 | type **12** background **k4**

color and **type**

color and **type**

932 | type **12** background **k5**

color and **type**

color and **type**

933 | type **12** background **k6**

color and **type**

color and type

934 | type **12** background **k7**

color and type

935 | type **12** background **k8**

color and **type**

color and **type**

936 | type **12** background **k10**

Because white reflects more light than any other color, it is generally an effective background choice for type. The intrinsic properties of any hue are best preserved when paired with white.

Observing how others solve the mysteries of color and type can be informative as well as inspiring, and it can open doors to new and exciting possibilities in your own work.

Using color and type

bserving how others solve the mysteries of color and type
n be instructional as well as inspiring, and it can open
ors to new and exciting possibilities in your own work.
eryone possesses different color sensibilities and opin-
ns, and a color scheme that works for one person is not
cessarily acceptable to another. No formula or single
ight" answer to any color and type problem exists. Sub-
quently, you have to make decisions based upon the
neless principle of *appropriateness.* This is to say that the
lution to a problem should always arise from within the
oblem and not outside of it. The following 30 case studies
present a wide range of printed applications and reveal
ow top designers address the problems of color and type.
u will find helpful tips throughout that will shed light on
ur own work.

rrowing from the collection of colors on pages 20 and 21,
lor swatches on the left-hand pages provide an approxi-
ation of the colors used in the examples, as well as the
antity and relative location of the colors within the design.
e purpose of these color swatches is to illustrate the
neral properties of the colors used in the projects. No
tempt is made to exactly duplicate the color schemes.
ese color combinations are keyed to the color conversion
art on page 154 for reference.

Design:
Jack Anderson
Heidi Favour
Mary Hermes
Mary Chin Hutchison
Julia LaPine
Hornall Anderson Design
Works, Inc.
Art Direction:
Jack Anderson

When the Print NW/Six Sigma company changed its name to Quebecor Integrated Media, they had an announcement designed to inform the public of the change. The announcement depicts three logos, each printed in black on vivid panels of both primary and secondary colors. Words describing the capabilities of the company are printed in a subtle, tinted varnish and extend across the entire announcement. This technique provides the piece with visual depth. Th same colors are used for stationery and other items, bringing unity to the entire program.

1

The chosen values of the colors ensure that black type remains readable when printed on top. Compare the varying levels of legibility of black type when printed on different values of a background color.

color and type	color and type
color and type	color and type
color and type	color and type

3

Stationery and binders are printed in the same palette of colors for a unified look.

2

The secondary colors of green, orange, and violet blend effectively with a primary blue to produce a pleasing collection of hues. The effect of the colors is striking, communicating energy and vision. The physical position of the colors in the announcement is very important for the overall effect. This example illustrates how the color effect changes as the position of hues is altered.

k10

t59

t45

4

t30

Typeface: Futura

Quebecor: Turning Technology Into Solutions.

1.800.451.5742

Your single source for Media delivery services.

An Integrated network of manufacturing facili

Design:
Bob Dinetz
Art Direction:
Bill Cahan
Cahan & Associates

Trident Microsystems designs, develops, and markets multimedia video processing chipsets, GUI accelerators, and graphics controllers. The annual report presented here communicates the company's achievements in this technology and in the marketplace. An animated message imitating a video screen changes from *FOLLOW* to *LEAD* as the reader shifts the cover from one position to another. The technologies that position the company for success are featured inside the annual report through an array of video images and an intensely bright palette of colors.

1

The word *LEAD* is repeated again on the first page of the report to reiterate the company's position as a leader. The word consists of orange letters with red outlines, a technique that creates emphasis and visual prominence.

LEAD

2

The three elements of the company's success – capabilities, relationships, and design – are presented in three interior spreads. A detail from one of these spreads shows a unique use of color and type. Appearing on top of a video image, the numeral *3* appears in three variations. These include the *3* with a black shadow, a red outline, and outlined in white. These numerals are stacked on top of one another but offset slightly for an energetic and vibrating appearance.

3

The letter to stockholders uses color to emphasize key information. Heads appear in black type of a bold weight, while highlighted information appears in red. The rest of the letter is printed in black type of a regular weight.

LETTER TO   *STOCKHOLDERS*

4

For financial charts, yellow ruled lines offer a subtle but effective alternative to commonly used black ruled lines.

Typefaces: Din Schriften, Univers

FLEADW

The cover, printed in a dazzlingly saturated yellow, cannot be ignored. This color combined with the lead/follow message entices the reader into the pages of the annual report.

CAPABILITIES

Design:
Stephen Doyle
Gary Tooth
Drenttel Doyle Partners

TIP: To create energy and dimensionality in your publication, use a combination of warm and cool colors for type and background.

Typography 16, the annual of the Type Directors Club, seduces the reader into its pages with risky typography and color. The designers state: "We wanted anyone interested in type to zoom in on this in a bookstore. . .not being able to figure it out, they would then pick it up." Indeed, at first glance the jacket appears to be an unruly hodgepodge of letterforms stacked indiscriminately on top of one another. But closer examination reveals a masterfully articulated structure and a lyrical dialogue between warm and cool hues of varying values and intensities.

1
A detail taken from the jacket reveals the subtle transparent effect created by overlapping transparent inks. Colors become darker and more neutral at the point of intersection.

2
A detail from the flap of the book's jacket reveals a single block of text type printed over three different background colors. The pastel text, appearing to float delicately above the surface of the paper, is darker or lighter in value depending on which of the colors it overlaps.

3
This sample page reveals text blocks of different shapes and colors pieced tightly together like a puzzle. The illusion of depth is created by warm and cool, advancing and receding colors. Each block features biographical information about the judges of the competition, and the varying shapes and colors of the blocks provide each with a unique personality. In the spirit of risk-taking, some of the text blocks offer challenging reading due to the colors assigned to them.

The only annual devoted exclusively to typographic design, Typography 16 presents the finest work in this field from 1994. Selected from 2,894 international submissions to the forty-first Type Directors Club competition (TDC41), the 239 winning designs are models of excellence and innovation in contemporary type design.

This year's selection encompasses a wide range of categories, among them posters, logotypes, packaging, promotions, books, stationery, magazines, television graphics, annual reports, videos, and corporate identities. Entries are displayed in full color and are accompanied by informative captions listing the designer, client, typography, and more.

The Judge's Choice section features the winning entries from the year's competition that have been singled out by each of the seven judges as his or her

k10	
s21	
k2	
s6	
t38	
s48	

4
The typographic forms found on the cover are reintroduced in a new variation on the title spread.

Typefaces: Didot, Matrix Script, Orator, Rockwell, Scala

TYPOGRAPHY

16

1995

THE
ANNUAL
OF THE

TYPE DIRECTORS CLUB

EXHIBITION
ST

The typography on the jacket is simultaneously chaotic and orderly, a blend of intentions that raises the reader's curiosity. While the letterforms are precisely arranged, sized, and aligned, their overlap creates a complex maze, a varied garden of shape and color through which the eye wanders.

Booklet

Piet Mondrian was an abstract painter whose theories about color and space were the basis of an art and design movement called de Stijl – an important movement that originated in Holland in 1917. Mondrian's paintings were reduced to straight lines, squares, rectangles, and the colors red, yellow, green, blue, black, white, and gray. This booklet, which features the work of Mondrian, explores and emulates the visual vocabulary of the artist.

1

On the cover, alternating primary hues suggest the color cadence of a Mondrian painting. Title typography possesses a similar rhythmic structure.

p i e t
m o n d r i a n
p a i n t   a n d   p r o c e s s

2

A detail from the contents page reveals a playground of type and color. Words are transformed into an intriguing visual pattern by the strategic insertion of red and yellow letters. We are reminded of the careful articulation of Mondrian's own forms.

c o n t e n t s

1	youth + education
2	process
3	abstraction
4	time line
5	maturity
6	bibliography
7	colophon

3

In a detail from a timeline within the booklet, words assigned primary colors emphasize the content.

1 9 4 0 — 4 4   continues to develop paintings; compositions reach an unrivaled intensity i composition of line, plane , and color

w
k10
k7
9
5
1

Typefaces: Helvetica, Serifa

A collection of spreads reveals Mondrian's preference for pure hues, especially the primaries red, yellow, and blue. Typography is placed horizontally and vertically, a formal trait characterizing the rectilinear energy of Mondrian's paintings.

Design:
Rob Carter
Rob Carter Design

ARTNOW is a series of exhibitions spon- taining the name of the featured artist, and a
sored by the Montgomery Museum of Fine four-color reproduction of the artist's work.
Arts. Brochures are designed to tie events Colors for each brochure reflect those used by
together as a series and to provide a consis- the artist. This approach not only helps to dis-
tent visual look. Design elements for the tinguish each of the brochures, it also informs
brochures include an identifying logotype the reader about the specific color palettes.
used for the series title, a vertical bar con-

Brochure

Place type and images on
black backgrounds if you wish
to create visual drama. Most
any color harmonizes with
black.

TIP:

1

The red *T* in the *ARTNOW*
logotype emulates the red in
the cover painting. The color
also provides the mark with
visual distinction and makes
the word *ART* more readable.
Compare the logotype with
and without the red *T*.

2

While only a hint of red
exists on the cover, a full-
bleed sea of the hue on the
back cover dazzles the reader. Compare the white head-
line and caption on the back
cover to the rest of the text,
which is set in black. A
heightened contrast between
the white letters and the red
background projects these
elements forward in space,
giving them hierarchical
prominence.

3

In the process of determining
which colors should be used
for the logotype, several
combinations were tested. A
few of the possibilities are
exhibited here. The version
with a red *T* was chosen for
its visual impact.

t43

1

k10

Typefaces: Franklin Gothic, Helvetica

A vertical bar containing the artist's name casts the same hue as in the painting. Extracting color from the cover painting and applying it to various typographic elements provides visual unity. Simultaneously, the juxtaposition of hot red and cool blue hues provides a resonant contrast.

When type and photographs containing light hues are placed upon black backgrounds – as in this cover – the entire space glows.

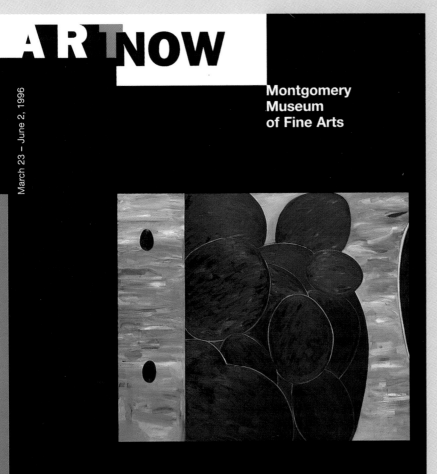

ART NOW

Montgomery
Museum
of Fine Arts

March 23 – June 2, 1996

John L. Moore

Design:
Jack Anderson
David Bates
Mary Hermes
John Anicker
Mary Chin Hutchison
Hornall Anderson Design
Works, Inc.
Art Direction:
Jack Anderson
Illustration:
Yutaka Sasaki
Photography:
Tom Collicott

TIP: To emphasize elements such as words and phrases within text, try using colors that contrast with the main body of the text. For more emphasis use stronger contrast and for less emphasis use weaker contrast.

NEXTLINK specializes in the next wave of telecommunications services, focusing specifically upon local phone service customers who desire telecommunications reliability and up-to-date technology. Distinctive typography, custom lettering, and bold colors provide the company with a visual identity program that projects a highly progressive image. The company operates flexibly. . . one foot in the future.

1

The logotype suggests the futuristic outlook of the company. A gradation beginning with red-violet and ending with yellow-orange travels through the space age letters of **NEXTLINK**. The letter *X* – a metaphor for a communications link – casts a shadow as it rises into new technological realms. Unlike the rest of the letters of the logotype, the *X* is carved from a curved plane of rainbow color.

NE▨TLINK

2

The *X* is most dramatic as it appears on the cover. Diecut through each page of the brochure, it forms a window from front to back. As the brochure is held to light, the *X* glows brilliantly. The background is silent and black, a deep space through which the *X* travels.

9
12
4

k10

3

Within the brochure, black text type is punctuated with yellow-orange call-outs that stress important points.

NETWORK AND COMPLETE SWITCHING ENVIRONMENT, ALLOWING OUR PARTNERS TO TEST DIFFERENT SERVICES AT NO RISK. THIS KIND OF COMMITMENT TO THE FUTURE IS JUST WHAT YOU'D EXPECT FROM A COMPANY THAT PLANS TO HELP TAKE YOUR ORGANIZATION'S TELECOMMUNICATIONS TO THE NEXT LEVEL.

4

The style and weight of text type reversed from photographs help to maintain legibility.

Typefaces: Eagle Book, Gill Sans

OUR PROMISE

To provide our customers
with real choices,
total solutions, and superior
telecommunications service.

IF YOU COULD CREATE A TELECOMMUNICA-
TIONS COMPANY FROM THE GROUND UP,
YOU WOULD MAKE CUSTOMER SERVICE
AS IMPORTANT AS TELEPHONE SERVICE.
YOU'D TREAT YOUR CUSTOMERS AS
BUSINESS, NOT JUST SOMEONE YOU SEND
BILLS TO. YOU'D PROVIDE SOLUTIONS, NOT

JUST SERVICES. YOU'D OFFER EXCEL-
LENT VALUE, NOT JUST COMPETITIVE
PRICES. YOU'D BUILD A SYSTEM YOU
COULD UPDATE EASILY, SO YOUR
CUSTOMERS WOULD ALWAYS HAVE THE
LATEST TECHNOLOGY AND GREATEST
RELIABILITY. WE'RE NEXTLINK. AND
THAT'S EXACTLY WHAT WE'RE DOING.

WE PROVIDE TOTAL TELECOMMUNICATIONS SOLUTIONS

• Customers Define Our
  Working Relationship

• Services and Pricing
  Tailored to Your Needs

• True Single Source
  Telecommunications

NEXTLINK is dedicated to the proposition that not all customers
are created equal. That each one has **UNIQUE NEEDS** that
require individual solutions. And that the right combination of
telecommunications products and services provides a **BUSINESS
ADVANTAGE**. You're probably not used to this approach. That's
understandable - traditional phone companies provide telephone
service. We provide **TELECOMMUNICATIONS SOLUTIONS**

Our way of working is anything but traditional. In fact, we're out to
redefine the entire customer-telecommunications company relationship. We start by working to understand not just your telecommunications needs but also your **TOTAL BUSINESS**. Then we develop
a complete solution that can include local exchange service, long
distance service, voice messaging, and high-speed data networks. All
from a **SINGLE SOURCE**. And we work around your schedule.
Your requirements. Your definition of success. Refreshing, isn't it?

• Real Partnership: Long-
  term Business Approach

• We Create and Identify
  Business Opportunities

OUR CUSTOMER COMMITMENT

• 24-hour Customer
  Service

• Dedicated Personal
  Service Representatives

• Meeting and Exceeding
  Customer Expectations

• Round-the-Clock
  Teleconferencing Centers

It takes a lot more than self-healing fiber networks to provide
reliable telecommunications service. It takes **PEOPLE**. People
who understand what it means to truly **SERVE** customers,
not just simply respond to them. People who take the time to
UNDERSTAND YOUR BUSINESS, so they can help you
run it better. People who turn technology into a **COMPETITIVE
ADVANTAGE** for you. The very people you'll find at NEXTLINK.

History teaches us that **BUSINESS** is full of surprises. But it
doesn't have to be. When you're a NEXTLINK customer, your problems
are our problems. Our success is directly tied to **YOUR SUCCESS**.
We're committed to building our business systems around your needs,
not ours. And the biggest surprise is discovering how pleasant life is
without unpleasant surprises. That's our approach. Because that's what
it takes to move telecommunications into the **NEXT CENTURY**

Each spread of the brochure
contains a photograph cast-
ing a specific tertiary hue.
The *X* whose background
reflects the hues contained
within the photographs is on
the right-hand page, adjacent the photographs.

Brochure

The purpose of this three-fold brochure is to demonstrate the capabilities of Dupli-graphic as a high-quality, two-color printer. Colors used for the brochure are a primary metallic blue (the corporate color) and black. Ink is applied to only one side of a translucent sheet, and when folded, the type and images peer through to the other side as well. A smiling woman wearing sun glasses encourages the reader to "take a look" at the capabilities of the printer. Together, the type, images, color, translucent paper, and folds create an intriguing and mirror-like message.

1
As demonstrated by the typo-graphic configuration on the inside of the brochure, a tremendous variety of type and color effects is possible using only two colors. Here we see type printed in two different solid colors, reversed from these colors to appear as white, and printed with screen mixes of the two colors to create a variety of tones.

type type
type type
type type
type type

2
When reversing type from solid color backgrounds, a number of factors affect legibility. Among these is the weight of type. Letter strokes, serifs, and punctuation of overly light type can appear too light; the counters (spaces within letters, such as in the lowercase e) of letters in heavy type may appear too small for adequate letter definition. Aggravating this problem is the printing phe-nomenon known as ink squeeze, where ink oozes over the edges of letter strokes and further thins them. Generally, medium weight type is most legible when reversed from solid color backgrounds. Compare the legibility of light, medi-um, and bold type reversed from identical color backgrounds.

color and type

color and type

color and type

3
Creating outline and solid rectangular shapes in each of the two colors to enclose type blocks contributes to the variety of the brochure.

s43

k10

Typefaces: Akzidenz Grotesk, Akzidenz Grotesk Extended

Design:
William Kochi
Kode Associates, Inc.

Black and white and the achromatic grays can appear amazingly colorful when light and dark values are effectively utilized. Similar to walking in a winter garden, the bright colors of summer yield to subtle hues playing upon faded foliage. The LinoGraphics Capabilities brochure is printed entirely in black ink on translucent paper. Type and images converse through layers of pages for a highly textured and tactile reading experience.

1

Remarkable variety can be achieved in type by using screens of black in different combinations. Note the stimulating, shimmering effect of these variations. Typographic legibility depends upon the amount of value contrast incorporated into each combination.

color and type   color and type   color and type

color and type   color and type   color and type

color and type   color and type   **color and type**

color and type   **color and type**   color and type

color and type   color and type   color and type

2

For a chart on the last page of the brochure, black type, white type on black and gray backgrounds, overlapping type, and type with generous letter spacing combine to create an active, vibrant texture.

3

Outlined type, graphic icons, ruled lines, and photographs mingle in harmony and contribute to the brochure's appeal.

k10

Typeface: Imago

e cover and inside cover
eal how type and images
nted on both sides of the
eet can be viewed simul-
eously. As viewed from
front, black elements
nted on the opposite side
pear gray, creating a rich
ality and a separation of
ments.

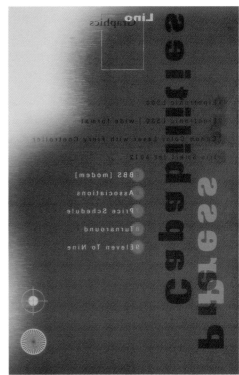

election of spreads from
brochure reveals a rich
nd of black and white and
ys. Despite the apparent
mplexity of the pages, type
d images remain readable
e to a careful orchestra-
n of color values. At the
me time, serendipity
des the interaction of
lor and type.

Art Direction:
Dana Lytle
Kevin Wade
Planet Design Co.

The intent of this retail catalog is to convey the elegance and style associated with the Saris products, which are roof rack systems for bicycles, skis, canoes, and other recreational equipment. The type is playful to allude to the sports of cycling, skiing, and paddling, but it also reflects the technical aspects of precision storage rack systems. The color palette consists of primary and secondary hues and is both sophisticated and funky.

1

Each page of the Saris catalog features a different background color. These are presented as circular blends that "spotlight" the products from page to page. For this catalog only one color was needed for the circular blends, but it is possible to combine different colors for a variety of effects.

2

At the tops of pages, running heads consisting of type on black bars make it easy for the reader to navigate the catalog. The type is printed in the same color as the background, creating the dimensional effect that it is cut away from the black bar to expose the underlying background.

Saris   hitch racks

3

On the back cover, an animated phrase is printed in both black and the yellow-green background color. Because the yellow-green letters appear over light areas of the same color blend, they remain readable; however, they are very subtle, receding quietly into space.

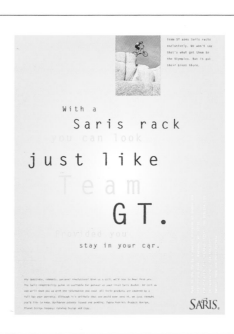

k10
s21
4
t39
s22
t44

Typeface: Letter Gothic

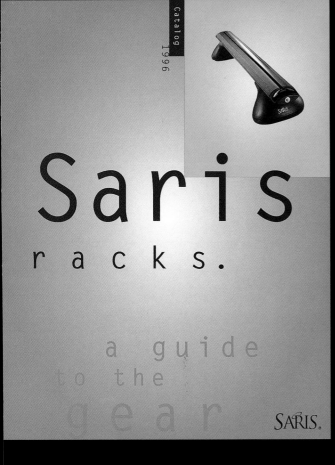

Saris
racks.

a guide
to the
gear

SARIS.

Each page of the catalog is a kinetic and rather complex organization of elements. Product images and type appear in constant motion, swirling about one another in space. Despite the seeming randomness of the pages, the size and color of the type elements and images establish a clear hierarchy. Product information appears as light gray patches of text type, while product names appear in large, black type. Product numbers, also large in size, are printed in white for immediate recognition.

Design:
Clifford Stoltze
Tracy Schroder
Heather Kramer
Peter Farrell
Resa Blatman
Stoltze Design

TIP: Don't be timid about taking daring chances with color and type. In this way you can discover color combinations that stand out and make an unforgettable statement. Do be sure, however, to select color that is appropriate to the needs of the design problem.

Through design and color, the Massachusetts College of Art catalog emulates a highly charged and experimental learning environment. Both primary and secondary hues present images and type, and they are shifted in value and saturation for a most unusual palette.

Flipping through the pages reveals an intriguing kaleidoscope of shapes, colors, and typographic treatments. Never a dull moment, the catalog parts with convention yet remains accessible and informative.

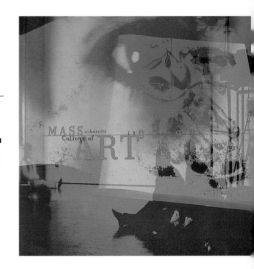

1

Consisting of black and hot, red type, the title thrusts forward from the background, which is a photographic montage with a muted yellow cast. The catalog's spine is blue. A detail of the cover shows the distribution of the title colors. Appearing in red, *MASS ART* is separated from *Massachusetts College of Art* to reveal the abbreviated pronunciation of the college's name.

2

Many risks are taken with color and type that defy legibility standards, but given the experimental nature of the institution, this is quite acceptable. The left example shows small, yellow-green text type printed over a red photograph. Though not easy to read, with effort the type is nonetheless readable. The context of a message and the intended audience are always important aspects to consider before testing the limits of typographic legibility. For the most part, the youthful audience of this catalog will have little trouble reading this text. The right example is a more normative page containing information that the reader must easily access.

3

In this detail we see how color and type are manipulated into a visual metaphor. The word *students* presents a kaleidoscope of colors, referring to the word *kaleidoscopic.*

4

Part of the charm of this publication is the tapestry of overlapping and layered type, color, and images.

k10

s22

2

t45

Typefaces: Calvino, Scala

Representative spreads
display a wild, exuberant
collection of colors, textures,
shapes, and letterforms.

Design:
John T. Drew
Sarah Meyer

Acuity 1.0 presents a system for determining the distance at which letterforms and symbols can be seen in any color combination for standard vision. Signifying the process of seeing, the image of an imposing human eye provides a visual centerpiece for the CD cover. The background colors and the hues assigned to the typography are influenced by the colors composing the eye. Contrast is achieved by using highly saturated colors compared to the softer colors of the eye.

1

Printed in red, the title *Acuity* bisects the eye, stretching from the pupil to the edge of the cornea. The treatment of the title is in effect a demonstration of the principles of visual acuity. The chosen typeface, size, and color enable optimal readability of the word from a distance of 12 to 14 inches. Beyond this distance, the title is difficult to impossible to read. While the specific hue and intensity of the letters provide sufficient contrast for overall readability of the word, certain letters are more legible than others. The *A*, for example, is more legible than the *t*, for there exists more contrast between this letter and its surrounding background. In general, the use of red contributes to striking color schemes, and it is a hue that is rarely confused with other hues.

2

Icons used to drive the software are pictured on the CD cover. These chromatic images are designed to represent specific software tools and functions. Not only do these depictions provide a clue about what is found in the actual software, they add a visual richness to the cover. The icons represent the following software functions: motion, typeface, type size, lighting, eyesight, reflection, color, and calculation (left to right).

3

The contrast between the violet and orange parts of the background is heightened by a stairstep edge aligned to the row of icons at the top of the cover. The stairstep pattern not only focuses attention on the dissonance between the two colors, it references the "building block" process unique to the software tools.

4

Pure red and violet stand one color apart on the color wheel for an analogous relationship. Text type on the CD cover appears in red on violet, a combination that is very harmonious. Due to lack of value contrast, however, combinations such as these should be used only for small amounts of text type. Compare the difference in legibility as the violet background progressively lightens in value.

red on violet

red on violet

red on violet

red on violet

red on violet

1

3

11

Typefaces: Gill Sans, New Baskerville Italic

A saturated palette of the
secondary hues of orange
and violet contrasts with the
muted tones of the eye image
(bottom). The CD also
incorporates the eye image
as it corresponds to the
overall design concept (top).

Design:
Mark Minelli
Pete Minelli
Lesley Kunikis
Brad Rhodes
Casey Reas
minelli design
CD Packaging Design:
Brad Rhodes

TIP: To achieve vibrant color and to multiply the actual number of colors available, try overprinting the transparent offset printing inks.

An interactive CD package for the Art Institute of Boston is part of a greater identity system for the school. Bold typography, enhanced and articulated through a slightly offbeat color palette, characterizes each component of the system. A number of hybrid colors were created by overprinting red, green, and purple inks, a technique that also aided the designers in overcoming budget limitations. The approach to color and type suggests the creative and experimental nature of the art school without abandoning the clarity of factual information.

1
As shown in this example, two solid colors can be combined to generate a third hybrid hue that provides richness and depth.

2
The colors used for the CD packaging are the same ones used for the interactive "buttons" featured in the CD itself. These buttons are selected with the mouse to navigate information about the school. Enough contrast exists between the hues to easily distinguish one from another.

3
A sleeve within the cover holds the CD. On this panel, violet is used for highly legible type; yellow-green is used for the image.

5
A darker color is used for the CD itself. This somber hue relates to poetic images encountered while interacting with the program.

4
Color is distributed among the letterforms in a manner reminiscent of an abstract painting. Though only three colors are actually used in the printing, reversing some letters to appear as white and printing others over a color background achieves the appearance of several colors.

t30

t59

1

Typefaces: Bodoni, Rockwell

the Art Institute of Boston

Interactive
CD-ROM

The
Art
Institute
of
Boston
Interactive
CD-ROM

Made with Macromedia is a
trademark of Macromedia, Inc.

Design:
Clifford Stoltze
Stoltze Design
Design Assistance:
Peter Farrell
Heather Kramer
Illustrators:
Various

Anon, a limited-edition compilation of art and music, includes two music CDs and a collection of 30 full-color postcards that are packaged in a natural cardboard container. Themes for the CDs are solar and lunar, which are introduced on the cover in the form of a diagram of the solar system. The two main colors used for the packaging are yellow for solar, silver for lunar, and black for text. The yellow and silver appear soft and delicate on their earthy background, an effect accentuated by flourishes of gently curving calligraphy.

1

On the cover, type and images printed in yellow, silver, and black overlap to create a complex and delicate motif. *Anon* is printed in black to clearly identify the title. Despite the complexity of the layers, each is clearly distinguished from the next.

2

A red-orange band binding the package together repeats the title, introduces the contents of the package, and brings warmth to the entire presentation.

3

Enlarged portions of the solar system diagram found on the cover and the title *Anon* in calligraphic letters are reversed from white to reveal the inherent silver cast of the CD.

k10

k3

5

Typefaces: Calvino, Gangly

he packaging is a statement
f contrasting forms, materi-
ls, and colors: the square
hape of the container and
e round diecut flaps
epresenting the sun and
oon; the raw neutrality of
e packaging material and
e elegance of the yellow
nd silver inks; and the title
non presented in both
urvilinear calligraphy and
ectilinear type.

Design:
**Jack Anderson
Lisa Cerveny
Jana Wilson
Suzanne Haddon**
*Hornall Anderson Design
Works, Inc.*
Art Direction:
Jack Anderson
Copy Writer:
Karen Wilson

TIP: Dynamic color relationships can be achieved by using colors nearly opposite one another on the color wheel, and then using a full range of tints and shades of those colors. In this way, the color palette is simultaneously congruent and incongruent.

For GNA Power Annuities, bold colors are used to depict the concept of "power." In fact, the design staff refers to specialty color mixes as Power Red, Power Orange, Power Gold, etc. These colors are forceful because of their intensity and slightly dark value. Also contributing to their strength is the extent to which they are used. Large, overlapping letters and numerals appearing in the power colors dynamically engage large areas of space within printed materials.

1
The large letters and numerals overlap one another with precision, subdividing the space into elegant, abstract shapes. The overlapping letters appear transparent as color changes in value at points of intersection.

2
While the same colors are used throughout the program, they are applied differently to each piece of communication. This technique not only establishes variety within the system, it helps to distinguish the various materials as well.

3
On the inside of a brochure, letters alternate in color to emphasize the word *POWER*.

4
For optimum readability, black text always appears on lighter values of the colors.

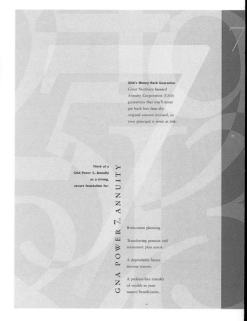

k10	
s28	
t54	
t20	
s3	
3	

Typefaces: MS Gothic, Sabon

The cover of a folder containing information about the company typifies the use of the power colors and the monumental letters and numbers that expand beyond the borders. This palette consists of the tertiary hues red-orange, yellow-orange, and red-violet.

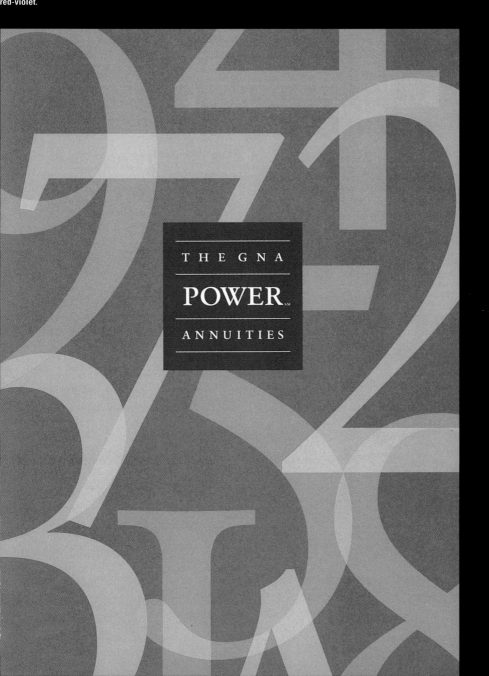

A photograph of sky and clouds serves as a poetic backdrop for this cover of *exp.* magazine. The sun establishes a dramatic focal point that draws attention to the magazine's vivid red title. The cottony appearance of the clouds provokes a strong contrast with rectilinear shapes that provide an organizational framework for the typography. The shapes appear as tinted glass panes with hues that intensify areas of the achromatic photograph. Juxtaposed with the sky, the color intensifies the illusion of three-dimensionality and creates a mood of contemplation and mystery.

TIP: Using transparent color provides an effective way of synthesizing type and photographs. However, be aware that an increase in transparency usually translates into a decrease in legibility. This technique works best for display rather than text type.

1

The computer enabled the designer to precisely adjust the color opacity in the rectangular shapes and letterforms. More opacity results in less transparency, while less opacity results in more transparency.

2

When reversing type from a background photograph, it is essential that the background is dark enough to ensure readability. This is a matter of contrast: if the background is too light, the type will appear too faint and therefore less readable.

3

Many different typographic manipulations can be used to separate and emphasize information, including the use of different typefaces and type weights. Assigning different colors to typographic parts is also an effective means to emphasize one element over another. Here, the word *Three* and the date *1996* achieve prominence through color.

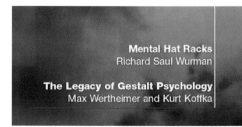

Mental Hat Racks
Richard Saul Wurman

The Legacy of Gestalt Psychology
Max Wertheimer and Kurt Koffka

4

A spread from the magazine's feature story utilizes the sky photograph, linking the cover and magazine interior. An image of a woman with the word *psychology* overlapping her forehead illustrates the topic of Gestalt psychology. The use of transparent color keeps the look of the magazine consistent.

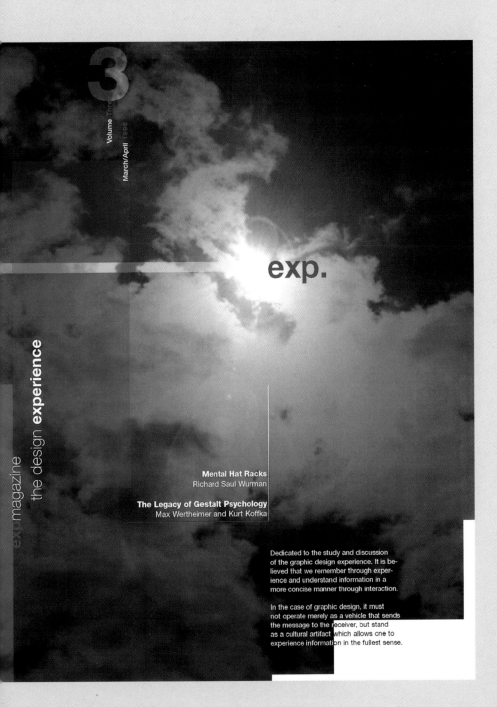

3

Volume Three

March/April 1998

exp.

exp. magazine

the design experience

Mental Hat Racks
Richard Saul Wurman

The Legacy of Gestalt Psychology
Max Wertheimer and Kurt Koffka

Dedicated to the study and discussion
of the graphic design experience. It is be-
lieved that we remember through experience and understand information in a
more concise manner through interaction.

In the case of graphic design, it must
not operate merely as a vehicle that sends
the message to the receiver, but stand
as a cultural artifact which allows one to
experience information in the fullest sense.

The primary purpose of this magazine advertisement is to demonstrate the high-quality printing capabilities of Dupli-Graphic. A closely cropped blue flower – exquisite, graceful, and subtly textured – serves as the ad's centerpiece. The ad is divided into halves; the top half contains the flower, and the bottom half displays a deep black field. The hardness of the black accentuates the flower's softness, and together the two parts form a rich and complementary whole. The flower and its blue hue suggest elegance, sophistication, and beauty.

Magazine advertisement

TIP: You can use typographic color as achieved through type style and spacing to give your design variety and vigor and to establish an ordered hierarchy among parts.

1
Within the ad's black rectangle, two blocks of text type reversed to appear as white are different in tone and luminescence. Referred to as typographic "color" (see page 33), any number of tones can be created by controlling typeface, type weight, spacing, and type size. In this example, text units differ distinctly in brightness and tone.

color and type

color and type

color and type

c o l o r   a n d   t y p e

2
At first glance the advertisement is a statement of blue and black only, but closer observation reveals a subtle yellow-green hue emanating from the center of the flower and in the letters *Dupli*. Finding relationships between even subtle colors within a design can provide nuance and color harmony.

3
Blue is also represented in Dupli-Graphic's logotype. The color begins at the top of a circle, and gradually fades as it moves in a clockwise direction. Together with the color gradation, the symbol abstractly refers to the printing process.

Dupli

w
s23
s43
k10

Typefaces: Akzidenz Grotesk, Akzidenz Grotesk Extended

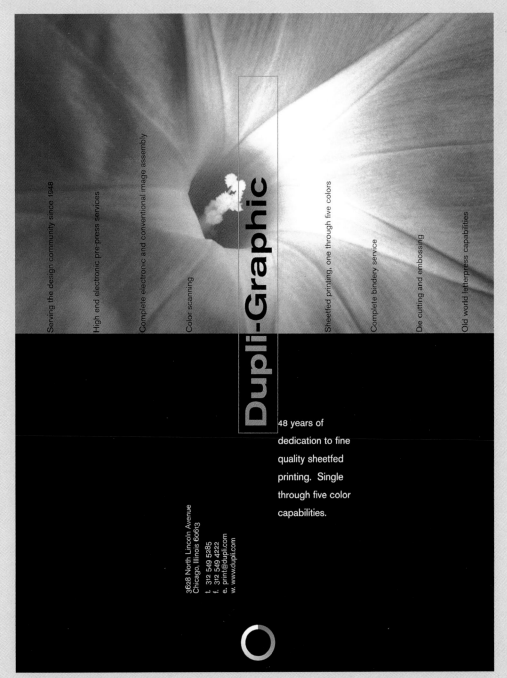

Where the advertisement's upper and lower halves join at the center, an edge is formed that establishes the design's central axis. Small lines of black type running vertically from the axis state the capabilities of the printing firm, unify the halves, and soften the hard edge.

Serving the design community since 1948

High end electronic pre-press services

Complete electronic and conventional image assembly

Color scanning

Dupli-Graphic

Sheetfed printing, one through five colors

Complete bindery service

Die cutting and embossing

Old world letterpress capabilities

48 years of dedication to fine quality sheetfed printing. Single through five color capabilities.

3628 North Lincoln Avenue
Chicago, Illinois 60613

t. 312 549 5285
f. 312 549 4222
e. print@dupli.com
w. www.dupli.com

Design:
Clifford Stoltze
Brett Snyder
Heather Kramer
Peter Farrell
Rebecca Fagan
Stoltze Design

When appropriate, choose color for type that mirrors the implied emotional and symbolic content of a message.

T I P :

Postcards designed by Stoltze Design express the meanings of significant words through the poetic use of color and type. Entitled *Presents of Mind,* the cards are sent to friends and clients. The series offers a marvelous collection of creative color and type effects generated on the computer.

Content used for the cards are dictionary definitions of the selected words. The three colors used for the postcards include a glowing, phosphorescent orange; a subtle, metallic bronze; and a deep, oceanic blue-green. These colors possess rare qualities and join with type in a lively, chromatic concert.

1

One sees a "spark" in overlapping letters and fragmented oblique shapes. The definition of spark as "something set off by a sudden force" is emphasized over other definitions by appearing in bright orange instead of blue-green.

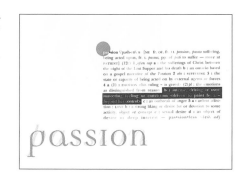

2

The word *passion* looks passionate through an emphatic layering of two contrasting typefaces and colors. "Flames" of passion appearing in the hot color flicker through a rectangular text block in cool blue-green.

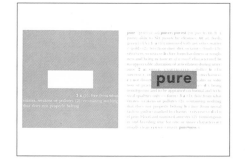

3

The concept of purity ("free from what vitiates, weakens, or pollutes") is established by extracting the word from its environment and placing it upon a different color within a new environment .

w

k2

s39

t10

A careful orchestration of overlapping elements demonstrates "harmony." Presenting the word in an elegant script and repeating it in a soft blend of mono-chromatic blue-greens reinforces the concept.

harmony

har·mo·ny \ˈhär-mə-nē\ *n pl* -nies [ME *armony* fr. MF *armonie* fr. L *harmonia* fr. Gk joint, harmony, fr. *harmos* joint — more at ARM] 1 *archaic* : tuneful sound : MELODY 2 a : the combination of simultaneous musical notes in a chord b : the structure of music with respect to the composition and progression of chords c : the science and the structure, relation, and progression of chords 3 a : pleasing or congruent arrangement of parts <a painting exhibiting ~ of color and line> b : CORRESPONDENCE, ACCORD <lives in ~ with her neighbors> c : internal calm : TRANQUILLITY 4 a : an interweaving of different accounts into a single narrative b : a systematic arrangement of parallel literary passages (as of the Gospels) for the purpose of showing agreement or harmony

Design:
Jean-Benoît Lévy
AND (Trafic Grafic)

The *A* stamp is the official priority mail stamp of the Swiss Post Office. Typically, expensive priority stamps are given warm colors while less expensive stamps are assigned cooler colors. For this stamp, Jean-Benoît Lévy decided to primarily employ warm colors but also to introduce cool colors for contrast. The edges of three interlocking shapes suggest an uppercase *A*. Stripes placed at the edges of the planes clearly define the letterform. The trilogy of shapes forming the letter *A* represents the three co-dependent parts of the mailing process: message, sender, and receiver.

1
The pinwheel shapes of the stamp appear substantially warmer and luminescent as they hover over a complementary cool blue sky. Within two of the shapes, linear color blends of red and yellow provide a shimmering effect.

2
Color blends and fades are effectively used in the stamp design. Easily achieved with a computer, this device modulates the surface of a form, providing a sense of three-dimensionality. As shown here, blends and fades come in several varieties, including linear, mid-linear, diamond, and rectangular.

3
Printed on an envelope is a simplified variation of the *A* form. Here, the structure of the stamp is clearly revealed. Moving clockwise, the shapes appear in an analogous gradation of red, orange, and yellow. This logical gradation provides cohesiveness and unity among the colors. The three functions of the mailing process are presented in converging upper-case letters printed over the three rectilinear shapes. These terms, presented in three languages, appear as three different but closely related hues.

4
The vivid warm colors and crisp geometric design of the *A* stamp give it distinction among other stamps.

Typeface: Futura

Design:
David Colley

TIP: If you are limited to the use of black, white, and gray, remember that these neutral colors work best when type and background contrast significantly in value, and that type set as a darker value on a lighter value works better than the inverse.

An opera poster for *Ariadne auf Naxos* comes to life in a rhythmic orchestration of type and color. This poster demonstrates how color may serve both as a means to emphasize and de-emphasize parts of information and to symbolically portray content. The poster is divided into two zones: a top zone consisting of a warm gray rectangle and robust typography that introduces the event; and a bottom zone with additional information set in text type and a painting by Titian called *Bacchus and Ariadne*. The painting portrays the classical myth surrounding the content of the opera.

1

The name *Richard Strauss* and the title *Ariadne auf Naxos* appear together on the warm gray rectangle in approximately the same size. Making one of these elements white and the other black creates a subtle distinction in emphasis. As the black unit advances in space, the white unit recedes (top). When both elements are assigned the same color, they are nearly equal in emphasis (bottom).

Richard Strauss
Ariadne auf Naxos

Richard Strauss
Ariadne auf Naxos

2

This example demonstrates how as the background changes in value, the type elements change in emphasis.

Richard Strauss
Ariadne auf Naxos

Richard Strauss
Ariadne auf Naxos

Richard Strauss
Ariadne auf Naxos

3

Below the gray rectangle, a painting by Titian entitled *Bacchus and Ariadne* portrays the classical myth upon which the opera is based. The painting is split horizontally into halves with the top half printed in black and white, and the bottom half printed in full color. This device represents the two distinct acts of the opera – two related but separate parts. The first act is a discussion among the actors about writing and producing an opera; the second act is a performance by the actors of the opera discussed in the first act. The black and white division of the painting signifies the unrealized production; the full-color component suggests the operatic event in real time.

k3
k10
w

Typefaces: Garamond, Univers

Sinfonia
da Camera
Ian Hobson, music director

Ian Hobson, *conductor*
Nicholas DiVirgilio, *director*

Richard Strauss
Ariadne auf Naxos
A comic, chamber opera

Saturday March 30 1996 at 8:00pm
Foellinger Great Hall
Krannert Center for the Performing Arts
University of Illinois at Urbana-Champaign
Ticket information: 217 333-6280

This performance is made possible through
the generosity of Richard and Rosann Noel.

Sinfonia da Camera appears under the auspices of the
University of Illinois at Urbana-Champaign in
association with the School of Music and the College
of Fine and Applied Arts.

The warmth of Titian's hues
is reflected in the warm gray
rectangle housing the title
information. Using colors
that possess similar properties helps to establish visual
unity within a design.

The richness and brilliance
of the four-color image is
pronounced by the predomi-
nantly black, white, and gray
surroundings. This vivid
contrast not only brings
visual impact to the poster, it
also strengthens the underlying concept of the split
image.

painting: Titian: *Bacchus and Ariadne*, 1520-23, National Gallery, London
design: David Colley
printing: Dupli-Graphic/Chicago

TIP: Use only the number of colors in a design that are absolutely necessary. If in doubt about the number, use as few as possible. A three-ring circus of color may entertain, but it will unlikely do little to enhance and augment the intended message.

A poster for color studies in the Department of Design at Ohio State University demonstrates an interaction of two colors through color blends. The background progresses from red to blue, with the transition occurring at the center of the poster. A second, smaller field of color inverts the relationship, progressing from blue to red. The transition of this blend occurs also at the center. Through this color exercise, the essence of the poster's content is stated.

1

Because it is neutral, the white type on the background does not interfere with the rest of the color on the poster. Any other color would have changed the intended effect, which is to emphasize the red and blue blend. Compare the two examples shown here.

Notice how the addition of type in a third hue changes the effect and perception of the two background colors and therefore changes the entire color statement.

2

Perhaps the most intriguing aspect of the poster is the simultaneous interaction of the color blends and the new hue resulting from their mix. Aside from the pure delight of color blends, they can (given an appropriate context) signify change, transition, time, and movement. An array of blends are pictured here; study the hue resulting from the interaction of the first two hues.

Typeface: Helvetica

Deeper Into Color

simultaneous contrast   vibration   transparency

programmed color   medial color

studies in complex color relationships in the Department of Design at the Ohio State University

TIP: If you are limited to the use of two colors, consider using a hue of darker value for type, and a hue of lighter value for background. This combination will optimize readability.

For this poster announcing a summer program in architecture at Columbia University, designer Willi Kunz uses color to organize and structure the poster's space. Suggesting architectural spaces, yellow and black geometric forms asymmetrically frame the poster and house information related to the program. Resting above an image of New York City, a circular sphere suggesting the sun signifies the season in which the program is offered. The overall effect of the color is warm and optimistic.

1

Although the black shape functions as a container for text type, it has a life and purpose of its own due to the strength of the black and the character of the shape. The boldness of the shape also calls attention to the information contained within it. Type can be placed into shapes of all kinds. Never, however, should the shapes distract from the message; they should in fact relate to it in some way. This shape refers to the architectural theme of the poster.

2

The juxtaposing arrangement of the black and yellow shapes (shown only as black shapes in the diagram) creates a third white shape. Together these interlocking forms establish the poster's organizational structure.

3

An effective transition from yellow to white is made in the poster by means of an intermediate series of yellow and white stripes. These alternating stripes read as a lighter yellow and soften the contrast between the yellow and white parts of the poster. Such transitions are often needed to bridge one color to another.

4

A light gray plane thrusting diagonally through the poster overlaps the sun motif and yellow shapes at the borders. This gives the plane a film-like, transparent quality.

w

k1

5

k10

Typeface: Univers

Columbia University
Graduate School of Architecture
Planning and Preservation

Introduction to Architecture

A Summer Studio in New York

A summer program giving university credit which introduces the student to aspects of the design, history, theory, and practice of architecture. The program is intended both for those without previous academic experience in design who are interested in architecture as a potential career, and for those with previous experience in architectural design who would like to develop additional studio design skills, perhaps in preparation for application to graduate school.

Courses are given in the studios of Avery Hall, home of Columbia University's world-renowned Graduate School of Architecture, Planning, and Preservation, on the Morningside Heights campus in New York City. Studios and seminar courses are taught by experienced architects and designers, coordinated and supervised by members of the faculty of the Graduate School. For those who may require it, housing is available on the University campus, with direct access to Avery Hall.

Students attend classes four days a week for five weeks, both morning and afternoon sessions. In the morning session, students are introduced to the fundamentals of architectural history and theory, structures, technology, and professional practice. Also, this course will introduce the student to the extraordinary city of New York, with its world famous collection of museums, cultural institutions, and architectural monuments. Lectures, seminar presentations, tours of architect's offices, and field-trips to active building sites, museums, and famous works of architecture in New York City are led by the instructors.

In addition, students will attend a series of special lectures to be given by distinguished and renowned architects, including the following:

Kenneth Frampton
Architect; professor; author of "Modern Architecture: A Critical History"

Steven Holl
Architect; professor; winner of numerous Progressive Architecture Awards

James Stewart Polshek
Architect; professor; designer for the renovation of Carnegie Hall

Robert A. M. Stern
Architect; professor; author of "Pride of Place"

Bernard Tschumi
Architect; Dean, Columbia University; designer of the park "La Villette", Paris

In the afternoon, the students attend the design studio — an educational method unique to architecture — a place where students are given an intensive training in the skills and critical thinking involved in architectural design. Students, in small groups, work directly with studio instructors to develop their individual designs, which the students then present in periodic reviews or "juries", where they hear the comments and criticism of the invited architects and professors. The design projects given in studio are frequently situated in New York City, so that the student is able to apply the knowledge he or she has gained from the morning sessions. The development of supporting skills such as drawing and model-building is also included in the studio curriculum.

Together the studio and lectures present a comprehensive introduction to every aspect of architecture as it is practiced today. In addition, through the various field-trips and tours, the student learns from the extraordinary examples of architectural and urban design in New York City, the world's preeminent center for architectural culture.

Program Director:
Thomas Hanrahan,
Architect, professor

Introduction to Architecture:
July 6 to August 6
Monday, Tuesday, Wednesday, Thursday
10:00am–5:00pm
3 credits, studio and seminar
Tuition for 1992: $1590
Housing on the Columbia University campus (if required): approximately $800

Applications should include a transcript of the applicant's academic record, a resume summarizing education, employment, and other types of experience; and, where appropriate, examples of the applicant's design work. Also please include a $35 application fee (checks made out to Columbia University).

Applications are due by June 30

For information and applications write or call:

Office of Admissions –
Introduction to
Architecture Program
Columbia University
Graduate School
of Architecture, Planning,
and Preservation
400 Avery Hall
New York, NY 10027
(212) 854-3414

Design:
John Malinoski

A poster for the Master of Fine Arts program at Virginia Commonwealth University defies the limitations of using only two colors. The basic palette – yellow and black – represents the school's colors. This color combination is always very attractive, an attribute that is further enhanced through inventive spacing, screening, and layering of typographic elements. Indeed, this poster displays a wealth of two-color possibilities, and in doing so expresses the seriousness, involvement, and energy of the educational program.

1
While many typographic conventions are pushed aside for the sake of playful experimentation, critical information is set in black to preserve legibility.

2
In spite of the textured layering of type and color, black retains fidelity on the yellow-orange. Make note of how the heavier type appears black, and how the the lighter type appears gray.

3
A pattern of horizontal lines creates the effect of a lighter value of yellow-orange and draws attention to the adjacent photograph.

w

4

k10

Typeface: Univers

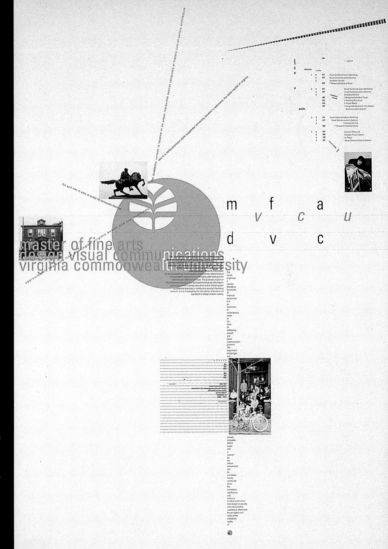

A large yellow dot provides a focal point for the poster. Lines of type radiate outward from the dot to encourage a search for information. While on the journey, color, type, and photographs give the reader a taste of the experiences offered by the program.

Design:
Nancy Skolos
Thomas Wedell
Skolos/Wedell
Photography:
Thomas Wedell

TIP: Black and red are always an excellent choice when limited to two colors. The stability of black and the energy of red offer a resonant contrast. From Renaissance books to modern advertising, this combination is ubiquitous and time tested.

This poster announces an exhibition that documents all 85 major shows of Marcel Duchamp's work. Because Duchamp was obsessed with the game of chess, this topic became the theme of the poster. Each of the show openings are set into blocks of type suggesting chess pieces and placed strategically around a metaphorical chess-board. The poster's typographic border is a repeated pattern of the word *DADA* used by Duchamp for a poster design for one of his shows in 1953.

1
The show listings, placed at various angles throughout the poster, appear in various combinations of red, black, and white. Unique use of color and type activates the space and supports the DADA theme of the poster. This detail reveals some of these combinations.

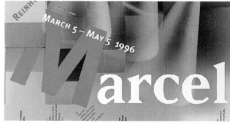

2
The border of the poster demonstrates a stimulating use of color and type. The letters *D* and *A* in the name *DUCHAMP* are slightly enlarged and assigned the color red. As the letters are repeated along the edges of the poster, the term *DADA*, the name of an art movement of the early 20th century, emerges.

3
Placed at identical angles, tucked behind forms within the underlying photograph, and presented in red, two large *M*s provide drama and focal points within the poster.

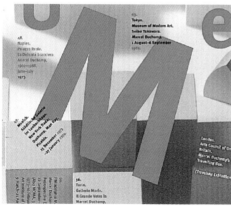

4
The large white letters in the name *Marcel* are carefully placed within the photograph to establish visual prominence. Placing the letters in a lighter section of the photograph would weaken them and render them less legible (see page 36).

W

k10

2

Typefaces: Keedy Sans, Matrix, Meta

Design:
Nancy Skolos
Thomas Wedell
Skolos/Wedell
Photography:
Thomas Wedell

Use color for typographic support elements such as ruled lines, bars, leaders, bullets, and other dingbats (assorted symbols used with a type font) to effectively flag and emphasize important information.

T I P :

The annual Lyceum Fellowship Competition is a travelling fellowship for undergraduate students in architecture. The 1996 program focuses on the house as a design problem, challenging students to think about the need to design a home rather than working with a generic set of developer's plans. A piece of yellow tracing paper with a site plan peels away from the skeletal structure of a home to visually reflect the architect's role in the design process. Yellow elevates the temperature of the poster, providing a mood of comfort and warmth.

1

The Lyceum logotype is superimposed onto yellow tracing paper. The transparent layers of the logotype represent the stages of conceptualization. Typefaces used for the logotype are Serifa and Futura. Serifa is collegiate in appearance; Futura refers to modern architecture. Folds in the tracing paper generate different values of yellow and create a distinct three-dimensionality related to architecture. The alternating yellow shapes in this example suggest a similar dimensionality and the illusion of a strong light source.

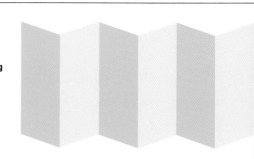

2

The general distribution of colors divides the poster into two interlocking shapes and creates a structural framework for type and images. The spatial divisions are active yet proportionally pleasing.

3

Yellow bars help to articulate the architectural structure and serve also as flags that mark typographic elements.

4

Black type on a yellow background proves highly visible and readable, a color combination frequently used in highway signage. In fact, black type reads well on any of the lighter warm hues. Black on red does not provide optimum legibility because these two colors are too close in value.

w

k10

t18

Typefaces: Futura, Meta, Serifa

Yellow and black effectively support the content. Adding other colors would only confuse the message or detract from the potency of just the black and yellow.

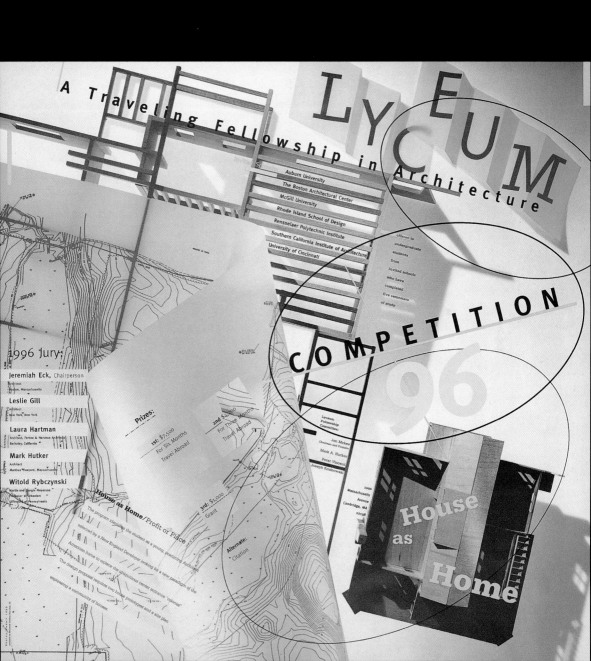

L Y C U M I

A Traveling Fellowship in Architecture

Auburn University
The Boston Architectural Center
McGill University
Rhode Island School of Design
Rensselaer Polytechnic Institute
Southern California Institute of Architecture
University of Cincinnati

offered to
undergraduate
students
from
invited schools
who have
completed
five semesters
of study

COMPETITION

96

1996 Jury:

Jeremiah Eck, Chairperson
Architect
Boston, Massachusetts

Leslie Gill
Architect
New York, New York

Laura Hartman
Architect, Fernau & Hartman Architects
Berkeley, California

Mark Hutker
Architect
Martha's Vineyard, Massachusetts

Witold Rybczynski
Martin and Margie Meyerson
Professor of Urbanism
University of Pennsylvania

Prizes:

1st: $7,500
For Six Months
Travel Abroad

2nd: $3,000
For Three Months
Travel Abroad

3rd: $1,000
Grant

Alternate:
Citation

Lyceum
Fellowship
Committee:

Jon McKee
Chairman and Founder

Mark A. Hutker

Peter Vincent

Joseph Szabowski

1000
Massachusetts
Avenue
Cambridge, MA
02138

House as Home/Profit or Place

The program considers the student as a young, practicing Architect
selected by a New England Developer looking for a new paradigm of the
American home to replace the ubiquitous center entrance "colonial."
The design proposal require two house prototypes and a site plan
expressing a community of houses.

House
as
Home

Design:
William Kochi
Kode Associates, Inc.
Photography:
William Kochi

When using color and type in publications, be consistent in the use of color for various typographic parts. For example, the small heads in this price guide are all presented in yellow.

T I P :

This small price guide provides a helpful resource for LinoGraphics customers, and it demonstrates the company's many capabilities. Each page offers a visual surprise with romantic, muted travel photographs and type mingling in a layered and textured conversation. The concept of "official" is parodied throughout the book: the cover is printed in an "official" cool gray; an "official" safety pattern delicately marks the left edge of each spread; and the "official" corporate seal, emblazoned in vivid red on the opening spread, is combined as a ghosted image in each of the interior photographs.

1
A stunning attribute of the book is the textures achieved by layering the photographs and typographic elements. Sufficient hue and value contrast preserves the integrity of each element.

2
Color can be used to link information from one page to another. These two pages reveal how letters of the word *GUIDE* appear on two different pages. *GU* (on the first page) and *IDE* (on the second page) are printed in black, linking them together. *IDE* is also cleverly integrated into the word *IDENTITY* on the second page.

3
The book reveals tremendous variety in form and color. Each page or spread features something unique, such as the overlapping red, green, and blue letters *RGB* on the RGB Scans page.

4
Used in tandem, the red ruled lines and the black type contribute to highly readable charts despite all the effusive visual activity of the pages.

w

k10

5

1

t43

Typefaces: OCR-B, Rockwell, Styvesant

The cover, printed in cool gray and simple in design, sets the reader up for a major sensory surprise. Upon opening the book, the pages bloom with activity and color. Juxtaposing neutral colors with highly chromatic colors can – when proportioned carefully – dazzle and delight the eye. A red colon at the right edge of the cover contrasts with the gray, appearing most luminescent because of its neutral surroundings. Though the smallest element on the cover, it is the most prominent. The mark is located in the same position and color on each spread, inviting the reader to turn to the next page (right).

On each spread the ghostlike remnants of the company's seal are reflected in computer-manipulated photographs (left).

Design:
David Collins
Judy Kirpich
Grafik Communications, Ltd.
Photography:
Pierre-Yves Goavec
Copy:
David Collins
Judy Kirpich

TIP: As in this publication, use special color effects for type only when they contribute in some way to the design concept. If used for no apparent reason, special effects clutter and dilute a typographic message.

This promotional booklet showcases the photographic work of Pierre-Yves Goavec. Short phrases on the left-hand pages refer to the dynamic oppositional forces found in Goavec's work. These pages gleam with primary, secondary, and tertiary hues related to the photographs. They are intended to keep the book colorful but not at the expense of the photographs themselves. The type is computer manipulated to give the impression of projected light, a well-known trademark of Goavec.

1

To create an impression of projected light, type is blurred and shifted out of focus. The background color invades and softens the normally hard edges of the letters. In addition, the monochromatic type elements overlap as if projected in layers upon a surface.

3

To reference the process of projected light, the letter *G* (for Goavec) on the cover is revealed as a sequence of small diecut dots through which light could theoretically pass to form a pattern of shimmering color. Except for a yellow band running along the left edge, the cover is exclusively white – perhaps a statement of white light.

4

On the back cover, a logotype for Pierre-Yves Goavec consists of a vertical red capsule with white uppercase letters. Vertical slashes that divide lines of type at the top and the bottom of the cover mimic this element. Referred to as visual correspondence, this use of color establishes relationships among parts of the design.

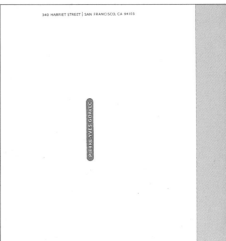

2

The computer can generate blurred type, a special effect that is greatly influenced by the colors used, for tonal gradations occur within the letters.

w

s42

s57

s2

10

s36

t20

Typefaces: Berkley, Myriad

Intensity
without
harshness

Randomness
without
chaos

Definition
without
edges

Three spreads from the booklet reveal the interrelatedness of the left- and right-hand pages. Colors for the left-hand pages are cued from the chromatic mix of colors in the adjacent photographs.

Design:
Nathan Lambdin

The design and color of this 45 RPM record album are sympathetic to the music of Minnow, the band featured on the album. Ambiguous and irregular shapes, an unusual typeface called Democratica, and a poetic organization of elements reflect the unique structure of Minnow's songs. Highly contrasting colors refer to the mood changes in the music. On the cover, small photos of numerals affixed to the band's instruments suggest a musical countdown (05, 04, 03, 02, 01) and contribute to the overall resonance of the design.

TIP:

Before selecting color, consider the moods and symbols it suggests. A few symbolic references are presented here:

Red: active, youthful, intense
Orange: exciting, spontaneous
Yellow: kinetic, upbeat
Green: fresh, healthy, hopeful
Blue: calm, trusting, strong
Violet: magical, imaginative

1
The emotion and mood of the band's music are established by the use of a split complementary color scheme. As described in chapter 2, this color scheme consists of a color and one or both of the colors on either side of its complement. Split complementary schemes are highly dynamic, as illustrated by the examples shown here. While only variations of the pure hues are shown, value adjustments in the colors would boost legibility when working with type.

2
Within the contrasting setting of split complementary colors, the use of very similar analogous hues such as orange, yellow, and yellow-green add a touch of subtlety and precision, another earmark of the band's music.

3
The two sides of the album cover are unified by reintroducing each of the split complementary colors as type. For example, the name *Minnow* appears on the yellow background in deep blue, while small text type appears in yellow on the blue. This weaving of color is illustrated in the diagram below.

4
5
s46

Typeface: Democratica

minnow

01

tod davis
nathan meltz. vocals
patrick.bass.
daniel.guitar.

b

a

3.4 the meaning of wings to fly

recorded by ricky
tubb.dec.1995. a spe-
cial thanks to patrick
kavanagh of buck for the
printing of this cover and to everyone who has
helped us in one way or another. contact minnow at 1208 a franklin st. richmond va.
23220. (804) 353-7751

Design:
Jack Anderson
David Bates
Hornall Anderson Design
Works, Inc.
Art Direction:
Jack Anderson

Stationery

Cf2GS is the acronym for the lengthy marketing communications firm's name Christiansen, Fritsch, Giersdorf, Grant, and Sperry, Inc. The creative use of the *2* for the two partners whose names begin with *G,* the innovative use of upper- and lower-case letters, and the incorporation of expressive color make this stationery system both unique and memorable. The elements of the logotype can appear in a serious and formal setting or in a more playful environment as purposes dictate.

T I P :

1

The colors used for the letters of the logotype consist of warm gray, cool gray, and bright yellow. The yellow glows in the midst of the more neutral hues, acquiring a strong presence and providing the mark with distinction. Without the contrasting yellow hue, the color would be lackluster at best.

2

Contrasts of hue, value, and intensity infuse a design with visual vitality. Shown from left to right is a composition that progresses from monochromatic elements to the addition of tints and finally to the addition of different hues and values. In the last example, color harmony is achieved through the juxtaposition of the two warm elements and the two cool elements.

 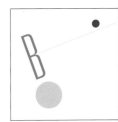

3

Typically, letterforms lie upon a stage of black, each acting out assigned roles (left). Sometimes, however, the letters behave playfully. Compare the front and back of the business card. To emphasize each partner equally, the largest letter of the last name is accentuated through size and position.

4

For variety, background colors for stationery items alternate between the three established hues. For example, on the back of the letterhead, the background shifts from black to cool gray. The numeral *2,* which is normally presented in white, now appears in black.

MARKETING
COMMUNICATIONS

DAVID GIERSDORF

1008
WESTERN AVE
SUITE 201
SEATTLE, WA
98104

206 223-6464
FAX 223-2765

CHRISTIANSEN FRITSCH GIERSDORF GRANT AND SPERRY, INC.

DAVID GIERSDORF

w

t20

k1

k4

k10

Typefaces: Bodoni, Caslon, Futura, Copperplate

Design:
Mark Meyer
Mark Oldach Design, Ltd.

The season program for the Steppenwolf Theatre Company reverberates with startling color and typographic virtuosity. Contrasting combinations of tertiary colors appear in great variety throughout the program, echoing the drama and excitement of the theatre. Typographic treatments are painstakingly resolved, appearing as a cast of well-rehearsed and talented characters. The reader is held captive by the energy and wit of this publication.

TIP: As illustrated in this program, energy, rhythm, and variety can be achieved within a publication if the specific concentration and allocation of color varies and shifts from page to page.

1
Selected spreads reveal the eloquent variety of the color and type.

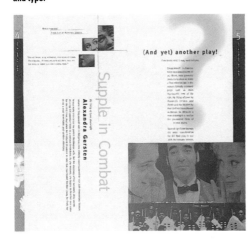

2
The typographic configuration introducing the play *Everyman* demonstrates a crafted unification of type, image, and color. Divided into two colors – white and blue-violet – the title is both resonant and readable. Note also the precise alignments of the type and image.

3
A subscription form on the last page of the program uses color to organize information. Zoning type with color in this way makes the form easier to complete.

4
Plays presented within the program are identified by a system of vertical bands. The bands, split into two colors, contain the number and dates of each play.

Typeface: Meta, Reactor

20 years of **Steppenwolf.
From out of our mind to
IN YOUR FACE

Steppenwolf Theatre Company
20th Anniversary Season
1995–96

TheLibertine

AMERICAN PREMIERE!
A PLAY BY STEPHEN JEFFREYS

Acclaimed Steppenwolf actor

John Malkovich

returns to the Chicago stage in this trenchant, witty portrait of the Earl of Rochester, the raconteur who inspired Etheridge's classic play "Man of Mode."

The Earl of Rochester delights in ravaging the noble fools of 1660's London with his rapier wit and merciless cynicism. His escapades with wine and women bring him celebrated notoriety, but he is not at all prepared to find truth and beauty in the world in the form of a young and talented actress—whose treachery may surpass even his own.

"I AM THE CYNIC OF OUR GOLDEN AGE. THIS BOUNTEOUS DISH WHICH OUR GREAT CHARLES AND OUR GREAT GOD HAVE PLACED BEFORE US SETS MY TEETH PERMANENTLY ON EDGE."

PHOTO: BRIGITTE LACOMBE

Yellow-green and blue-violet split an image of John Malkovich, intensifying the already provocative image. Typographic elements frame the eyes of the actor, calling attention to his piercing gaze.

Colorful wall graphics were designed to create public awareness of a historic site owned by The Council for America's First Freedom. This site will be the location of a reconstruction of Virginia's first capitol, a religious freedom study center, and a monument to religious freedom. At this location in 1786, Thomas Jefferson's Statute for Religious Freedom was approved by the Virginia General Assembly. This was the first time religious freedom was guaranteed to a people by law.

Wall graphics

TIP: If you wish to give selected typographic elements precedence over other elements in an environment of pure hues and shades, try dressing them in white. This will thrust them towards the viewer and imbue them with commanding visual strength.

1
The rectilinear shapes of the walls provide a structural framework for the organization of the color and typography. On this wall the most vivid element is a vertical red bar enclosing Thomas Jefferson's name. The words of the statute, set in justified Helvetica type with generous leading, are white against a blue-green background. This luminous typography commands attention and worthily presents the message's content.

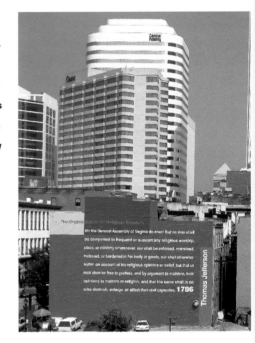

2
To avoid competition with the visual strength of the statute, the title typography is deliberately assigned less contrasting colors.

The Virginia Statute for Religious Freedom

We the General Assembly of Virginia do e
be compelled to frequent or support a
place, or ministry whatsoever, nor shall be
molested, or burdened in his body or good
suffer on account of his religious opinion

	W
	1
	s46
	5
	s37

3
Commemorating the reconstruction of Virginia's first capitol at this site, a replica facade was built and placed upon a warehouse wall. An enormous initial capital *O*, set in yellow upon a deep blue-green background, rises like the sun to focus the reader's attention upon historic facts.

Typeface: Helvetica

Monumental typography set upon blazing walls separates historic site buildings from the surrounding city environment. The pure hues of yellow, red, blue-green, and blue-violet provide startling contrast to the somber tones of the cityscape.

Color conversion chart

	c	m	y	k
■ s5	100	100		80
■ s4	100	100		70
■ s3	100	100		50
■ s2	100	100		30
■ s1	100	100		10
■ 1	100	100		
■ t5	90	80		
■ t4	70	65		
■ t3	55	50		
■ t2	30	30		
■ t1	20	15		
■ s10	80	100		80
■ s9	80	100		70
■ s8	80	100		50
■ s7	80	100		30
■ s6	80	100		10
■ 2	80	100		
■ t10	65	80		
■ t9	50	65		
■ t8	40	50		
■ t7	30	35		
■ t6	20	20		

	c	m	y	k
■ k10				100
■ k9				90
■ k8				80
■ k7				70
■ k6				60
■ k5				50
■ k4				40
■ k3				30
■ k2				20
■ k1				10
□ w				0

	c	m	y	k
■ s15	60	100		80
■ s14	60	100		70
■ s13	60	100		50
■ s12	60	100		30
■ s11	60	100		10
■ 3	60	100		
■ t15	50	80		
■ t14	40	65		
■ t13	30	50		
■ t12	20	35		
■ t11	15	20		

	c	m	y	k
■ s20	40	100		80
■ s19	40	100		70
■ s18	40	100		50
■ s17	40	100		30
■ s16	40	100		10
■ 4	40	100		
■ t20	30	80		
■ t19	25	65		
■ t18	20	50		
■ t17	10	35		
■ t16	5	25		
■ s25		100		80
■ s24		100		70
■ s23		100		50
■ s22		100		30
■ s21		100		10
■ 5		100		
■ t25		80		
■ t24		65		
■ t23		50		
■ t22		35		
■ t21		25		
■ s30	55	100		80
■ s29	55	100		70
■ s28	55	100		50
■ s27	55	100		30
■ s26	55	100		10
■ 6	55	100		
■ t30	40			80
■ t29	30			65
■ t28	20			50
■ t27	15			35
■ t26	10			20

	c	m	y	k
■ s35	85		85	80
■ s34	85		85	70
■ s33	85		85	50
■ s32	85		85	30
■ s31	85		85	10
■ 7	85		85	
■ t35	75		70	
■ t34	65		55	
■ t33	55		45	
■ t32	35		35	
■ t31	25		20	
■ s40	100		40	80
■ s39	100		40	70
■ s38	100		40	50
■ s37	100		40	30
■ s36	100		40	10
■ 8	100		40	
■ t40	90		35	
■ t39	70		30	
■ t38	55		25	
■ t37	40		20	
■ t36	25		10	
■ s45	100	55		80
■ s44	100	55		70
■ s43	100	55		50
■ s42	100	55		30
■ s41	100	55		10
■ 9	100	50		
■ t45	85	45		
■ t44	65	40		
■ t43	50	35		
■ t42	40	25		
■ t41	25	10		

	c	m	y	k
■ s50	100	85		80
■ s49	100	85		70
■ s48	100	85		50
■ s47	100	85		30
■ s46	100	85		10
■ 10	100	85		
■ t50	90	75		
■ t49	70	65		
■ t48	55	50		
■ t47	40	35		
■ t46	25	25		
■ s55	75	100		80
■ s54	75	100		70
■ s53	75	100		50
■ s52	75	100		30
■ s51	75	100		10
■ 11	75	100		
■ t55	60	85		
■ t54	45	70		
■ t53	35	55		
■ t52	25	40		
■ t51	15	30		
■ s60	40	100		80
■ s59	40	100		70
■ s58	40	100		50
■ s57	40	100		30
■ s56	40	100		10
■ 12	40	100		
■ t60	35	80		
■ t59	30	65		
■ t58	25	50		
■ t57	15	35		
■ t56	5	20		

AND (Trafic Grafic)
Spalenvorstadt 11
4051 Basel
Switzerland

Cahan & Associates
818 Brannan Street, Suite 300
San Francisco, California 94103

David Colley
2820 East Grace Street
Richmond, Virginia 23223

Drenttel Doyle Partners
1123 Broadway
New York, New York 10010

Ernest Bernhardi
Communication Arts and Design
School of the Arts
Virginia Commonwealth
University
P.O. Box 842519
Richmond, Virginia 23284-2519

Grafik Communications, Ltd.
1199 N. Fairfax Street, Suite 700
Alexandria, Virginia 22314

**Hornall Anderson Design
Works, Inc.**
1008 Western, 6th Floor
Seattle, Washington 98104

Hutchinson Associates, Inc.
1147 West Ohio, Suite 305
Chicago, Illinois 60622

John T. Drew
University of Utah
Department of Art
AAC 161
Salt Lake City, Utah 84112

John Malinoski
815 Jessamine Street
Richmond, Virginia 23223

Kode Associates, Inc.
54 West 22 Street
New York, New York 10010-5811

Mark Oldach Design, Ltd.
3316 N. Lincoln Avenue
Chicago, Illinois 60657

Minelli Design
381 Congress Street, 5th Floor
Boston, Massachusetts 02210

Nathan Lambdin
Communication Arts and Design
School of the Arts
Virginia Commonwealth
University
P.O. Box 842519
Richmond, Virginia 23284-2519

Philip B. Meggs
10211 Windbluff Drive
Richmond, Virginia 23233

Planet Design Co.
605 Williamson Street
Madison, Wisconsin 53703

Rob Carter Design
2920 Glendower Circle
Midlothian, Virginia 23113

Sarah Meyer
University of Utah
Department of Art
AAC 161
Salt Lake City, Utah 84112

Scott Allison
Communication Arts and Design
School of the Arts
Virginia Commonwealth
University
P.O. Box 842519
Richmond, Virginia 23284-2519

Skolos/Wedell
529 Main Street
Charlestown, Massachusetts
02129

Stoltze Design
49 Melcher Street
Boston, Massachusetts 02210

Willi Kunz Associates, Inc.
2112 Broadway
New York, New York 10023

Acknowledgments

While writing and designing this book, several people offered generous assistance. I deeply appreciate the designers whose excellent work appears in Chapter 5. Despite the rigors of professional practice, they took time to provide materials, information, and permissions for reproduction. At Virginia Commonwealth University, John DeMao, Chairman of the Department of Communication Arts and Design, provided encouragement and support. At Rotovision SA, Brian Morris, Managing Director, and Angie Patchell, Senior Art Director, provided encouragement and guidance. Colleagues Philip Meggs and John Malinoski offered advice about content and design. With intelligence and sensitivity, Diana Lively read and copyedited the book. Molly Carter and Mindy Carter read the manuscript and made insightful suggestions. Mindy Carter also compiled the index. I greatly appreciate the commitment to quality and excellence of Alice Goh, Eileen Thong, and staff at Provision Ltd., Singapore. They make beautiful books. George Nan contributed impeccable photographic work. Jerry Bates and Joseph Dimiceli helped to solve technical problems as they arose. My wife, Sally Carter, offered endless encouraging words and made me laugh during difficult phases of the project.

Working with Computer Type 3 was typeset and designed on a Power Macintosh 7100/66. Software used includes QuarkXPress, FreeHand, Illustrator, and PhotoShop. Text throughout the book is set in the Univers family.

color

&type